PENGUIN BOOKS

A FIELD GUIDE TO GETTING LOST

Rebecca Solnit is a writer whose work focuses on issues of environment, landscape, and place. She is the author of *Secret Exhibition: Six California Artists of the Cold War Era*; *Savage Dreams: A Journey into the Landscape Wars of the American West*; *A Book of Migrations: Some Passages in Ireland*; *Wanderlust: A History of Walking*; *Hollow City: The Siege of San Francisco and the Crisis of American Urbanism*; *As Eve Said to the Serpent: On Landscape, Gender, and Art*, which was a finalist for the National Book Critics Circle Award; *River of Shadows: Eadweard Muybridge and the Technological Wild West*, which was the winner of the National Book Critics Circle Award, the Mark Lynton History Prize, and the Sally Hacher Prize from the Society for the History of Technology; *Hope in the Dark: Untold Histories, Wild Possibilities* and, with Mark Klett and Byron Wolfe, *Yosemite in Time*. In 2003, she was the recipient of a Lannan Literary Award. She lives in California.

Praise for *A Field Guide to Getting Lost* by Rebecca Solnit

"Solnit is a writer to get lost in. . . . Her peregrine curiosity, not just from book to book but from page to page, is challenging in the best sense of the word. She grabs a reader by the hand and dares us to follow, but it's down to us to keep up with her. . . . For those readers who admire the play of Solnit's intelligence across any landscape—or no landscape at all—just the fumes from *A Field Guide to Getting Lost* can disorient you for days."　　　　　　　　*—San Francisco Chronicle*

"Solnit is a distinctive and original writer. . . . Her expressive, often beautiful writing finely conveys the force of her insights and vision. For the intrepid Blakean 'mental traveler' as well as for travelers of the physical realms, *A Field Guide to Getting Lost* is a book to set you wandering down strangely fruitful trails of thought."　　*—Los Angeles Times*

"I could have easily lost myself in this book for one hundred more pages. Solnit's work at its best is as fresh as an orange, for over the past dozen years this prolific Californian has produced a series of consis-

P9-CQD-347

tently provocative books.... *A Field Guide to Getting Lost* stands out for Solnit's willingness to push harder on her language than she has ever before.... Here she is far more personal, far more direct.... Her prose here glistens like a snake with a new skin."   —*The Nation*

"The paradox of loss as discovery, of finding oneself by losing oneself, is the subject—or, more accurately, the occasion—of *A Field Guide to Getting Lost*. ... Solnit's writing is both descriptive and meditative, and what we might loosely call lyrical or poetic, sometimes movingly evocative.... At its best, her writing evokes some of the great writers of the West, especially the desert and its denizens: Edward Abbey, Willa Cather, and, perhaps most of all, Mary Austin, with whom Solnit shares a feminist sensibility about the place of humans in the natural world."
                                                —*The San Diego Union-Tribune*

"An apprentice to the world at large, Solnit has made a life's work out of scavenging for connections.... Her essays sweep through myriad varieties of loss, from objects to memories to love, with plenty of slippage between the categories. She believes that losing things is intrinsic to human life, a never ending process of abandonment and discovery. ... *A Field Guide to Getting Lost* sometimes gets lost itself ... but even then, Solnit can catch the reader by surprise, illuminating some ordinary place we've all been so that suddenly we see the hidden possibilities embedded everywhere."   —*The Village Voice*

"Solnit's breakthrough book, *Wanderlust*, offered a clever cultural history of mankind and walking. Her latest book is an even more far-reaching meditation on the art of wandering—only now she has focused on travel without a destination.... It is a kind of self-help book for the philosophically inclined, its geography spanning the personal to the actual. ... Some of the loveliest writing in the book springs out of the rough soil of Solnit's own experience—where personal loss has been mulched down into melancholy and introspection, then replanted with something whimsical and skyward-reaching. ... The first place we must go to lose ourselves is the terra incognita of our minds, Solnit suggests time and time again, and this impractical but beautiful book provides a sort of compass for that trip. It's well worth squeezing into your pocket."   —*St. Petersburg Times*

"Solnit has written before about walking as a political experience, about the desert, and even about losing oneself and getting lost, but the interconnected essays in *A Field Guide* take flight from her own emblematic stories of childhood places, family members, friendship, urban ruins, madness or desert love, making this new work a kind of memoir that opens out again and again to encounter the unknown."

—*The Oregonian*

"Solnit is a conglomerating writer, melding borrowed history with contemplation, curiosity with a pastiche of facts, snatches of contemporary song with passages lifted from Dante. Many compare her with Susan Sontag but I tend to think she has more in common with Annie Dillard, whose thoughts often turn to the power of nature and whose prose is often graced with lyricism. . . . I have always admired Solnit for the subjects she tackles, for the great distances she travels, for the obscure books she reads, for her spirit. I have always loved the sound of her sentences."

—*The Baltimore Sun*

"In her new book, Solnit offers a compelling case for a state more commonly avoided than aspired to. . . . *Field Guide* aims both to give us the necessary education in existential abandon, and to explain the merits of this state of mind. . . . Solnit's concern with consciousness and identity opens a broad terrain. A writer could go in many different directions in describing the processes of losing the self and then finding it again. That's precisely what Solnit does. . . . The guiding intelligence of her essays recalls Annie Dillard, while her naturalist's affection for the southwestern desert and the Great Salt Lake are reminiscent of Terry Tempest Williams."

—*In These Times*

"Here Solnit ponders the Zen of getting lost in a lithesome essay collection. . . . She not only thinks innovatively and writes beautifully, she also trips the wire in the mind that hushes the static of routine concerns and allows readers to perceive hidden aspects of life, thus opening up new inner vistas for us to explore, even to the point of getting blissfully lost."

—*Booklist*

A

Field

Guide

to

Getting

Lost

-|||||||||||||||||-

Rebecca

Solnit

PENGUIN BOOKS

PENGUIN BOOKS

Published by the Penguin Group
Penguin Group (USA) Inc., 375 Hudson Street, New York, New York 10014, U.S.A.
Penguin Group (Canada), 90 Eglinton Avenue East, Suite 700, Toronto,
Ontario, Canada M4P 2Y3 (a division of Pearson Penguin Canada Inc.)
Penguin Books Ltd, 80 Strand, London WC2R 0RL, England
Penguin Ireland, 25 St Stephen's Green, Dublin 2, Ireland
(a division of Penguin Books Ltd)
Penguin Group (Australia), 250 Camberwell Road, Camberwell,
Victoria 3124, Australia (a division of Pearson Australia Group Pty Ltd)
Penguin Books India Pvt Ltd, 11 Community Centre,
Panchsheel Park, New Delhi – 110 017, India
Penguin Group (NZ), cnr Airborne and Rosedale Roads, Albany,
Auckland 1310, New Zealand (a division of Pearson New Zealand Ltd)
Penguin Books (South Africa) (Pty) Ltd, 24 Sturdee Avenue,
Rosebank, Johannesburg 2196, South Africa

Penguin Books Ltd, Registered Offices:
80 Strand, London WC2R 0RL, England

First published in the United States of America by Viking Penguin,
a member of Penguin Group (USA) Inc. 2005
Published in Penguin Books 2006

25   24   23   22   21   20   19   18   17   16

"Daisy Chain" in different form was published in *Tracing Cultures, Points of Entry: Volume III* (The Friends of Photography, San Francisco, 1995). A portion of "Abandon" (as "After the Ruins") appeared in *Art Issues*, November/December 2001.

THE LIBRARY OF CONGRESS HAS CATALOGED THE HARDCOVER EDITION AS FOLLOWS:
Solnit, Rebecca.
A field guide to getting lost / Rebecca Solnit.
p. cm.
ISBN 0-670-03421-5 (hc.)
ISBN 0 14 30.3724 2 (pbk.)
1. United States—Description and travel.   2. West (U.S.)—Description and travel.
3. Landscape—United States.   4. Landscape—West (U.S.)   5. Solnit, Rebecca—
Travel—United States.   6. Solnit, Rebecca—Travel—West (U.S.)
7. Travel—Philosophy.   8. Arts—Philosophy.   I. Title.
E169.04S628   2005
917.904'54—dc22   2004061241

Printed in the United States of America

A

Field

Guide

to

Getting

Lost

Open

Door

The first time I got drunk was on Elijah's wine. I was eight or so. It was Passover, the feast that celebrates the flight from Egypt and invites the prophet into the house. I was sitting at the grown-ups' table, because when my parents and this other couple joined forces there were five boys altogether, and the adults had decided that I was better off being ignored by their generation than mine. The tablecloth was red and orange, cluttered with glasses, plates, serving dishes, silver, and candles. I confused the stemmed goblet set out for the prophet with my own adjoining shot glass of sweet ruby wine and drank it up. When my mother eventually noticed, I lurched and grinned a little, but when she looked upset, I imitated sobriety instead of tipsiness.

She was a lapsed Catholic, and the other woman a former Protestant, but their husbands were Jews, and the women thought it good to keep up the custom for the kids. So the Passover glass of wine was set out for Elijah. In some versions, he will come back to earth at the end of time and answer all the unanswerable questions. In others, he wanders the earth in rags, answering difficult questions for scholars. I don't know if the rest of the tradition was followed and a door left open for him to enter by, but I can picture the orange front door or one of the sliding glass doors into the backyard of this ranch-style house in a small valley open to the cool night air of spring. Ordinarily, we locked doors, though nothing unexpected came down our street in this northernmost subdivision in the county but wildlife, deer tap-tapping on the asphalt in the early hours, raccoons and skunks hiding in the shrubbery. This opening the door to night, prophecy, and the end of time would have been a thrilling violation of ordinary practice. Nor can I recall what the wine opened up for me—perhaps a happier detachment from the conversation going on above me, a sense of limpidness in the suddenly tangible gravity of a small body on this middle-sized planet.

Leave the door open for the unknown, the door into the dark. That's where the most important things come from, where you yourself came from, and where you will go. Three years ago I was giving a workshop in the Rockies. A student came in bearing a quote from what she said was the pre-Socratic philosopher Meno. It read, "How will you go about finding that thing the nature of which is totally unknown to you?" I copied it down, and it has stayed with me since. The student made big transparent photographs of swimmers underwater and hung them from the ceiling with the light shining through them, so that to walk among them was to have the shadows of swimmers travel across your body in a space that itself came to seem aquatic and mysterious. The question she carried struck me as the basic tactical question in life. The things we want are transformative, and we don't know or only think we know what is on the other side of that transformation. Love, wisdom, grace, inspiration—how do you go about finding these things that are in some ways about extending the boundaries of the self into unknown territory, about becoming someone else?

Certainly for artists of all stripes, the unknown, the idea or the form or the tale that has not yet arrived, is what must be found. It is the job of artists to open doors and invite in prophesies, the unknown, the unfamiliar; it's where their work comes from, although its arrival signals the beginning of the long disciplined process of making it their own. Scientists too, as J. Robert Oppenheimer once remarked, "live always at the 'edge of mystery'—the boundary of the unknown." But they transform the unknown into the known, haul it in like fishermen; artists get you out into that dark sea.

Edgar Allan Poe declared, "All experience, in matters of philosophical discovery, teaches us that, in such discovery, it is the unforeseen upon which we must calculate most largely." Poe is consciously juxtaposing the word "calculate," which implies a cold counting up of the facts or measurements, with "the unforeseen," that which cannot be measured or counted, only anticipated. How do you calculate upon the unforeseen? It seems to be an art of recognizing the role of the unforeseen, of keeping your balance amid surprises, of collaborating with chance, of recognizing that there are some essential mysteries in the world and thereby a limit to calculation, to plan, to control. To calculate on the unforeseen is perhaps exactly the paradoxical operation that life most requires of us.

On a celebrated midwinter's night in 1817 the poet John Keats walked home talking with some friends "and several things dove-tailed in my mind, and at once it struck me what quality went to form a Man of Achievement, especially in Literature. . . . I mean Negative Capability, that is, when a man is capable of being in uncertainties, mysteries, doubts, without any irritable reaching after fact and reason." One way or another this notion occurs over and over again, like the spots labeled "terra incognita" on old maps.

"Not to find one's way in a city may well be uninteresting and banal. It requires ignorance—nothing more," says the twentieth-century philosopher-essayist Walter Benjamin. "But to lose oneself in a city—as one loses oneself in a forest—that calls for quite a different schooling." To lose yourself: a voluptuous surrender, lost in your arms, lost to the world, utterly immersed in what is present so that its surroundings fade away. In Benjamin's terms, to be lost is to be fully present, and to be fully present is to be capable of being in uncertainty and mystery. And one does not get lost but loses oneself, with the implication that it is a conscious choice, a chosen surrender, a psychic state achievable through geography.

That thing the nature of which is totally unknown to you is usually what you need to find, and finding it is a matter of getting lost. The word "lost" comes from

||||||

the Old Norse *los,* meaning the disbanding of an army, and this origin suggests soldiers falling out of formation to go home, a truce with the wide world. I worry now that many people never disband their armies, never go beyond what they know. Advertising, alarmist news, technology, incessant busyness, and the design of public and private space conspire to make it so. A recent article about the return of wildlife to suburbia described snow-covered yards in which the footprints of animals are abundant and those of children are entirely absent. As far as the animals are concerned, the suburbs are an abandoned landscape, and so they roam with confidence. Children seldom roam, even in the safest places. Because of their parents' fear of the monstrous things that might happen (and do happen, but rarely), the wonderful things that happen as a matter of course are stripped away from them. For me, childhood roaming was what developed self-reliance, a sense of direction and adventure, imagination, a will to explore, to be able to get a little lost and then figure out the way back. I wonder what will come of placing this generation under house arrest.

That summer in the Rockies when I heard Meno's question, I went on a walk with the students into a landscape I'd never seen before. Between the white columns of aspens, delicate green plants grew knee-deep, sporting leaves like green fans and lozenges and scallops, and the stems waved white and violet flowers in the breeze. The path led down to a river dear to bears. When we got back, a strong brown-skinned woman was waiting at the trailhead, a woman I'd met briefly a decade earlier. That she recognized me and I recalled her was surprising; that we became friends after this second meeting was my good fortune. Sallie had long been a member of the Mountain Search and Rescue team, and that day at the trailhead she was on a routine mission—one of those quests for lost hikers in which, she said, they usually reappear somewhere near where they vanished. She was monitoring her radio and watching to see who came up that trail, one of the trails the straying party was likely to appear on, and so she found me. The Rockies thereabouts are like crumpled fabric, a steep landscape of ridges and valleys running in all directions, easy to get lost in and not so hard to walk out of, down to the roads that run through the bottom of a lot of the valleys. For the search-and-rescue volunteers themselves, every rescue is a trip into the unknown. They may find a grateful person or a corpse, may find quickly or after weeks of intensive fieldwork, or never find the missing or solve their mystery at all.

Three years later I went back to visit Sallie and her mountains and ask her about getting lost. One day of that visit we walked along the Continental Divide on a path that rose from twelve thousand feet along ridgelines, across the alpine tundra carpeting the landscape above tree line. As we proceeded uphill, the view opened up in all directions until our trail seemed like the center seam of a world hemmed all around the horizon in rows of jagged blue mountains. Calling this place the Continental Divide made you picture water flowing toward both oceans, the spine of mountains running most of the length of the continent, made you imagine the cardinal directions radiating from it, gave you a sense of where you were in the most metaphysical if not the most practical sense. I would have walked forever into those heights, but thunder in the massed clouds and a long bolt of lightning made Sallie turn around. On the way down, I asked her about the rescues that stood out for her. One was about rescuing a man killed by lightning, not an uncommon way to die up there, which is why we were heading downhill from that glorious crest.

Then, she told me about a lost eleven-year-old, a deaf boy who was also losing his eyesight as part of a degenerative disease that would eventually cut short his life. He had been at a camp where the counselors took the kids on an excursion and then led them in a game of hide-and-seek. He must have hidden too well, for they could not find him when the day was done, and he did not find his way back. Search and Rescue was called out in the dark, and Sallie went into the swampy area with dread, expecting that in that nearly freezing night they could find nothing but a body. They blanketed the area, and just as the sun came over the horizon, she heard a whistle and ran toward it. It was the boy, shivering and blowing a whistle, and she hugged him and then stripped off most of her clothing to put it on him. He had done everything right—his whistle had not been loud enough for the counselors to hear above the running water, but he had whistled until nightfall, then curled up between two fallen trees, and begun whistling again as soon as it was light. He was radiant at being found, and she was in tears at finding him.

Search-and-rescue teams have made an art of finding and a science of how people get lost, though as many or more of their forays are rescues for people who are injured or stranded. The simplest answer nowadays for literal getting lost is that a lot of the people who get lost aren't paying attention when they do so, don't know what to do when they realize they don't know how to return, or don't admit they don't know. There's an art of attending to weather, to the route you take, to the landmarks along the way, to how if you turn around you can see how different the journey back looks from the journey out, to reading the sun and moon and stars to orient yourself, to the direction of running water, to the thousand things that make the wild a text that can be read by the literate. The lost are often illiterate in this language that is the language of the earth itself, or don't stop to read it. And there's another art of being at home in the unknown, so that being in its midst isn't cause for panic or suffering, of being at home with being lost. That ability may not be so far astray from Keats's capability "of being in uncertainties, mysteries, doubts." (Cell phones and GPS have become substitutes for this ability as more and more people use them to order their own rescues like pizza, though there are still many places without phone signals.)

Hunters get lost a lot in this stretch of the Rockies, Sallie's friend Landon told me, sitting at her desk surrounded by photographs of family and animals on the ranch she ran with her husband, because they routinely go off trail in pursuit of game. She told me about a deer hunter who glanced around on a plateau where the peaks in opposite directions look identical. Where he stood, one of those sets of peaks was obscured by trees, so he later traveled in exactly the wrong direction. Convinced that arrival was just over the next ridge or the next, he walked all day and night, exhausting himself and getting chilled and then, with the delusion of severe hypothermia, he began to feel hot and to shed his clothes, leaving a trail of garments they tracked him by for the last few miles. Children, Landon said, are good at getting lost, because "the key in survival is knowing you're lost": they don't stray far, they curl up in some sheltered place at night, they know they need help.

Landon talked about the old skills and instincts that people need in the wild and about her husband's uncanny intuition, which she saw as much one of those abilities as all the concrete arts of navigating, tracking, and surviving she studied. He had driven a snowmobile right up to the feet of a doctor lost when a warm winter walk turned into a whiteout, knowing by some unnameable instinct where the freezing man was, off the trail and across a snowed-over meadow. A ranch hand had commented on how strange another rescue had been because they had gone out into the snowy night silently, instead of calling. The rancher didn't call because he knew where he was headed, and he stopped on the brink of the ledge below which the skier was stuck. The lost skier had tried to follow the stream out, usually a good technique for navigating, but this stream narrowed and deepened until it was a series of waterfalls and precipitous drops. The skier had gotten stranded down a drop, huddled up with his sweater over his knees. The wet sweater was so frozen they'd almost had to chip him out of it.

I was trained by an outdoorsman who insisted you should always carry rain gear, water, and other supplies on the least excursion, that you should be prepared to be out for any amount of time, since plans go astray and the one certain thing about weather is that it changes. My skills are not notable, but I never seem to do more than flirt with getting lost on streets and trails and highways and sometimes cross-country, touching the edge of the unknown that sharpens the senses. I love going out of my way, beyond what I know, and finding my way back a few extra miles, by another trail, with a compass that argues with a map, with strangers' contrary anecdotal directions. Nights alone in motels in remote western towns where I know no one and no one I know knows where I am, nights with the strange paintings and floral spreads and cable television that furnish a reprieve from my own biography, when in Benjamin's terms I have lost myself though I know where I am. Moments when I say to myself as feet or car clear a crest or round a bend, I have never seen this place before. Times when some architectural detail or vista that has escaped me these many years says to me that I never did know where I was, even when I was home. Stories that make the familiar strange again, like those that revealed the lost landscapes, lost cemeteries, lost species around my home. Conversations that make everything around them disappear. Dreams that I forget until I realize they have colored everything I felt and did that day. Getting lost like that seems like the beginning of finding your way or finding another way, though there are other ways of being lost.

Nineteenth-century Americans seldom seem to have gotten lost as disastrously as the strays and corpses picked up by search-and-rescue teams. I went looking for their tales of being lost and found that being off course for a day or a week wasn't a disaster for those who didn't keep a tight schedule, knew how to live off the land, how to track, how to navigate by heavenly bodies, waterways, and word-of-mouth in those places before they were mapped. "I never was lost in the woods in my whole life," said Daniel Boone, "though once I was confused for three days." For Boone the distinction is a legitimate one, since he could eventually get himself back to where he knew where he was and knew what to do betweentimes. Sacajawea's celebrated role on the Lewis and Clark expedition wasn't primarily that of a navigator; she made their being lost more viable by her knowledge of useful plants, of languages, by the way she and her infant signified to the tribes they encountered that this was not a war party, and perhaps by her sense that all this was home, or somebody's home. Like her, a lot of the white scouts, trappers, and explorers were at home in the unknown, for though the particular place might be unfamiliar to them, the wild was in many cases their chosen residence. Explorers, the historian Aaron Sachs wrote me in answer to a question, "were always lost, because they'd never been to these places before. They never expected to know exactly where they were. Yet, at the same time, many of them knew their instruments pretty well and understood their trajectories within a reasonable degree of accuracy. In my opinion, their most important skill was simply a sense of optimism about surviving and finding their way." Lost, these people I talked to helped me understand, was mostly a state of mind, and this applies as much to all the metaphysical and metaphorical states of being lost as to blundering around in the backcountry.

The question then is how to get lost. Never to get lost is not to live, not to know how to get lost brings you to destruction, and somewhere in the terra incognita in between lies a life of discovery. Along with his own words, Sachs sent me a chunk of Thoreau, for whom navigating life and wilderness and meaning are the same art, and who slips subtly from one to the other in the course of a sentence. "It is a surprising and memorable, as well as valuable, experience to be lost in the woods any time," he wrote in *Walden*. "Not till we are completely lost, or turned round,—for a man needs only to be turned round once with his eyes shut in this world to be lost,—do we appreciate the vastness and strangeness of nature. Not till we are lost, in other words, not till we have lost the world, do we begin to find ourselves, and realize where we are and the infinite extent of our relations." Thoreau is playing with the biblical question about what it profits a man if he gains the whole world and loses his own soul. Lose the whole world, he asserts, get lost in it, and find your soul.

"How will you go about finding that thing the nature of which is totally unknown to you?" I carried Meno's question around with me for years and then, when everything was going wrong, friends came bearing stories, one after another, and they seemed to provide, if not answers, at least milestones and signposts. Out of the blue, May sent me a long passage by Virginia Woolf she'd copied in round black letters on thick unlined paper. It was about a mother and wife alone at the end of the day: "For now she need not think about anybody. She could be herself, by herself. And that was what now she often felt the need of—to think; well, not even to think. To be silent; to be alone. All the being and the doing, expansive, glittering, vocal, evaporated; and one shrunk, with a sense of solemnity, to being oneself, a wedge-shaped core of darkness, something invisible to others. Although she continued to knit, and sat upright, it was thus that she felt herself; and this self having shed its attachments was free for the strangest adventures. When life sank down for a moment, the range of experience seemed limitless. . . . Beneath it is all dark, it is all spreading, it is unfathomably deep; but now and again we rise to the surface and that is what you see us by. Her horizon seemed to her limitless."

That passage from *To the Lighthouse* echoed something of Woolf's I already knew, her essay about walking that declared, "As we step out of the house on a fine evening between four and six, we shed the self our friends know us by and become part of that vast republican army of anonymous trampers, whose society is so agreeable after the solitude of one's room. . . . Into each of these lives one could penetrate a little way, far enough to give one the illusion that one is not tethered to a single mind, but can put on briefly for a few minutes the bodies and minds of others." For Woolf, getting lost was not a matter of geography so much as identity, a passionate desire, even an urgent need, to become no one and anyone, to shake off the shackles that remind you who you are, who others think you are. This dissolution of identity is familiar to travelers in foreign places and remote fastnesses, but Woolf, with her acute perception of the nuances of consciousness, could find it in a stroll down the street, a moment's solitude in an armchair. Woolf was not a romantic, not a celebrant of that getting lost that is erotic love, in which the beloved becomes an invitation to become who you secretly, dormantly, like a locust underground waiting for the seventeen-year call, already are in hiding, that love for the other that is also a desire to reside in your

||||||||

own mystery in the mystery of others. Her getting lost was solitary, like Thoreau's.

Malcolm, apropos of nothing at all, brought up the Wintu in north-central California, who don't use the words *left* and *right* to describe their own bodies but use the cardinal directions. I was enraptured by this description of a language and behind it a cultural imagination in which the self only exists in reference to the rest of the world, no you without mountains, without sun, without sky. As Dorothy Lee wrote, "When the Wintu goes up the river, the hills are to the west, the river to the east; and a mosquito bites him on the west arm. When he returns, the hills are still to the west, but, when he scratches his mosquito bite, he scratches his east arm." In that language, the self is never lost the way so many contemporary people who get lost in the wild are lost, without knowing the directions, without tracking their relationship not just to the trail but to the horizon and the light and the stars, but such a speaker would be lost without a world to connect to, lost in the modern limbos of subways and department stores. In Wintu, it's the world that's stable, yourself that's contingent, that's nothing apart from its surroundings.

I never heard of a stronger sense of place and direction, but that directional consciousness is embedded in a language almost lost. A decade ago there were six to ten speakers of Wintu, six people fluent in a language in which the self was not the autonomous entity we think we are when we carry our rights and lefts with

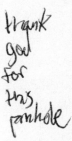
thank you for this panhole

us. The last fluent speaker of northern Wintu, Flora Jones, died in 2003, but the man who e-mailed me that information, Matt Root, mentioned that three Wintu people and one Pit River neighbor "retain fractions of the old Wintu slang and pronunciation system." He himself studied the language and hoped that it would be revived, so that his people would "begin to make connections with their past through our language. The Wintu world view is indeed unique, it is our intimacy with our habitat that complements this uniqueness, and it is thru the eventual reintroduction of people, place, culture, and history that will begin to heal the long held scars of removal and outright genocide. The precursors to the loss of language today." Or as a recent article about the hundred rapidly vanishing indigenous languages of California put it, "Such language differentiation may be tied to ecological differentiation. In this view, people adapted their words to the ecological niches they occupied, and California's highly varied ecology encouraged its lingustic diversity. The theory is supported by maps indicating that areas with greater numbers of animal and plant species also have greater numbers of languages."

It would be nice to imagine that the Wintu were once so perfectly situated in a world of known boundaries that they had no experience of being lost, but their neighbors to the north, the Pit River or Achumawi people, suggest that this was probably not so. One day I went to meet friends at a performance in a city park, but when I could not find them in the crowd, I wandered into a used bookstore and found an old book. In it, Jaime de Angulo, the wild Spanish storyteller-anthropologist who eighty years ago spent considerable time among these people, wrote, "I want to speak now of a certain curious phenomenon found among the Pit River Indians. The Indians refer to it in English as 'wandering.' They say of a certain man, 'He is wandering,' or 'He has started to wander.' It would seem that under certain conditions of mental stress an individual finds life in his accustomed surroundings too hard to bear. Such a man starts to wander. He goes about the country, traveling aimlessly. He will stop here and there at the camps of friends or relations, moving on, never stopping at any place longer than a few days. He will not make any outward show of grief, sorrow or worry. . . . The Wanderer, man or woman, shuns camps and villages, remains in wild, lonely places, on the tops of mountains, in the bottoms of canyons." This wanderer isn't so far from Woolf, and she too knew despair and the desire for what Buddhists call unbeing, the desire that finally led her to walk into a river with pockets full of rocks. It's not about being lost but about trying to lose yourself.

De Angulo goes on to say that wandering can lead to death, to hopelessness, to madness, to various froms of despair, or that it may lead to encounters with other powers in the remoter places a wanderer may go. He concludes, "When you have become quite wild, then perhaps some of the wild things will come to take a look at you, and one of them may perhaps take a fancy to you, not because you are suffering and cold, but simply because he happens to like your looks. When this happens, the wandering is over, and the Indian becomes a shaman." You get lost out of a desire to be lost. But in the place called lost strange things are found, De Angulo's editor notes, "All white men are wanderers, the old people say."

shaman or death?

During this long spell when stories rained down, I gave a reading at a bar on a street that faced water before the shoreline was filled in to squeeze a few more blocks of city out of the north face of the San Francisco peninsula. I read a short piece that ended in a downpour and another one about the sea and then went to collect my drink. Carol, the wife of the man who'd invited me to read, waved me over to the bar stool next to her and wound up telling me about the tattoo artist who'd been their neighbor for many years. The tattoo artist was a junkie for decades, and then a scab on his hand from shooting up got infected. He ended up in the hospital with a near-fatal systemic infection, and they had to amputate his arm, his right arm, his working arm. But, to his amazement, at the end of that long period of going to the edge of death and coming back, the doctor told him he was cured of his addiction. He was thrown out of the hospital without his craft, but clean, starting from scratch, as abrupt and overwhelming an emergence into the world as birth. A dragon had been tattooed up that arm, and all but the head of the dragon was gone.

My friend Suzie told me while I was driving her

home from that bar about the real meaning of the blindfolded figure of Justice holding the scales. Suzie was drawing her own tarot cards and rethinking each card as she went. Justice, a book on classical lore asserted, stood at the gates of Hades deciding who would go in, and to go in was to be chosen for refinement through suffering, adventure, transformation, a punishing route to the reward that is the transformed self. It made going to hell seem different. And it suggested that justice is a far more complicated and incalculable thing than we often imagine, that if everything is to come out even in the end, then the end is farther away than anticipated and far harder to estimate. It suggests too that to reside in comfort can be to have fallen by the wayside. Go to hell, but keep moving once you get there, come out the other side. Finally she drew a group around a campfire as her picture of justice, saying that justice is helping each other on the journey. Another night, Suzie's partner David told told me about a Hawaiian biologist he met who discovers new species by getting intentionally lost in the rainforest. The density of foliage and overcast skies there make the task easier than in the plateau country of the Wintu.

David had been photographing endangered species in the Hawaiian rainforest and elsewhere for years, and his collections of photographs and Suzie's tarot cards seemed somehow related. Because species disappear when their habitat does, he photographed them against the nowhere of a black backdrop (which sometimes meant propping up a black velvet cloth in the most unlikely places and discouraging climates), and so each creature, each plant, stood as though for a formal portrait alone against the darkness. The photographs looked like cards too, cards from the deck of the world in which each creature describes a history, a way of being in the world, a set of possibilities, a deck from which cards are being thrown away, one after another. Plants and animals are also a language, even in our reduced, domesticated English, where children grow like weeds or come out smelling like roses, the market is made up of bulls and bears, politics of hawks and doves. Like cards, flora and fauna could be read again and again, not only alone but in combination, in the endlessly shifting combinations of a nature that tells its own stories and colors ours, a nature we are losing without knowing even the extent of that loss.

Lost really has two disparate meanings. Losing things is about the familiar falling away, getting lost is about the unfamiliar appearing. There are objects and people that disappear from your sight or knowledge or possession; you lose a bracelet, a friend, the key. You still know where you are. Everything is familiar except that there is one item less, one missing element. Or you get lost, in which case the world has become larger than your knowledge of it. Either way, there is a loss of control. Imagine yourself streaming through time shedding gloves, umbrellas, wrenches, books, friends, homes, names. This is what the view looks like if you take a rear-facing seat on the train. Looking forward you constantly acquire moments of arrival, moments of realization, moments of discovery. The wind blows your hair back and you are greeted by what you have never seen before. The material falls away in onrushing experience. It peels off like skin from a molting snake. Of course to forget the past is to lose the sense of loss that is also memory of an absent richness and a set of clues to navigate the present by; the art is not one of forgetting but letting go. And when everything else is gone, you can be rich in loss.

Finally I set out to look for Meno. I had thought that his question would be part of a collection of aphorisms or fragments, like the fragments of Heraclitus. I had a clear picture of a book that doesn't exist. If I'd ever known, I'd forgotten that Meno is the title of one of Plato's dialogues. Socrates faces off with the sophist Meno, and as always in Plato's rigged boxing contests, demolishes his opponent. Sometimes while walking I catch sight of what at a little distance looks like a jewel or flower and turns out a few steps later to be trash. Yet before it is fully revealed, it looks beautiful. So does Meno's question, though it might only be so in the flowery translation I first encountered, out of context. Socrates answers that question, "I know, Meno, what you mean; but just see what a tiresome dispute you are introducing. You argue that man cannot enquire either about that which he knows, or about that which he does not know; for if he knows, he has no need to enquire; and if not, he cannot; for he does not know the very subject about which he is to enquire."

The important thing is not that Elijah might show up someday. The important thing is that the doors are left open to the dark every year. Jewish tradition holds that some questions are more significant than their answers, and such is the case with this one. The question as the water-photographer had presented it was like a bell whose reverberations hang on the air for a long time, becoming quieter and quieter but never seeming to do something as simple as stop. Socrates, or Plato, seems determined to stop it. The question arises that arises with many works of art: does the work mean what the artist intended it to mean, does Meno's argument mean what he or Plato intended it to mean? Or is it larger than they intended? For it is not, after all, really a question about whether you can know the unknown, arrive in it, but how to go about looking for it, how to travel.

For most of the dialogue, Socrates rebuts and attacks Meno with logic and argument and even mathematics. But for this question he shifts into mysticism—that is, into unsubstantiatable and poetic assertion. After his first dismissive reply, he adds, "And they say—mark, now, and see whether their words are true—they say that the soul of man is immortal, and at one time has an end, which is termed dying, and at another time is born again, but is never destroyed. And the moral is, that a man ought to live always in perfect holiness. 'For in the ninth year Persephone sends the souls of those from whom she has received the penalty of ancient crime back again from beneath into the light of the sun above, and these are they who become noble kings and mighty men and great in wisdom and are called saintly heroes in after ages.' The soul, then, as being immortal, and having been born again many times, and having seen all things that exist, whether in this world or in the world below, has knowledge of them all . . . all enquiry and all learning is but recollection." Socrates says you can know the unknown because you remember it. You already know what seems unknown; you have been here before, but only when you were someone else. This only shifts the location of the unknown from unknown other to unknown self. Meno says, Mystery. Socrates says, On the contrary, Mystery. That much is certain. It can be a kind of compass.

What follows are a few of my own maps.

jesus.

The

Blue

of

Distance

The world is blue at its edges and in its depths. This blue is the light that got lost. Light at the blue end of the spectrum does not travel the whole distance from the sun to us. It disperses among the molecules of the air, it scatters in water. Water is colorless, shallow water appears to be the color of whatever lies underneath it, but deep water is full of this scattered light, the purer the water the deeper the blue. The sky is blue for the same reason, but the blue at the horizon, the blue of land that seems to be dissolving into the sky, is a deeper, dreamier, melancholy blue, the blue at the farthest reaches of the places where you see for miles, the blue of distance. This light that does not touch us, does not travel the whole distance, the light that gets lost, gives us the beauty of the world, so much of which is in the color blue.

For many years, I have been moved by the blue at the far edge of what can be seen, that color of horizons, of remote mountain ranges, of anything far away. The color of that distance is the color of an emotion, the color of solitude and of desire, the color of there seen from here, the color of where you are not. And the color of where you can never go. For the blue is not in the place those miles away at the horizon, but in the atmospheric distance between you and the mountains. "Longing," says the poet Robert Hass, "because desire is full of endless distances." Blue is the color of longing for the distances you never arrive in, for the blue world. One soft humid early spring morning driving a winding road across Mount Tamalpais, the 2,500-foot mountain just north of the Golden Gate Bridge, a bend reveals a sudden vision of San Francisco in shades of blue, a city in a dream, and I was filled with a tremendous yearning to live in that place of blue hills and blue buildings, though I do live there, I had just left there after breakfast, and the brown coffee and yellow eggs and green traffic lights filled me with no such desire, and besides I was looking forward to going hiking on the mountain's west slope.

We treat desire as a problem to be solved, address what desire is for and focus on that something and how to acquire it rather than on the nature and the sensation of desire, though often it is the distance between us and the object of desire that fills the space in between with the blue of longing. I wonder sometimes whether with a slight adjustment of perspective it could be cherished as a sensation on its own terms, since it is as inherent to the human condition as blue is to distance? If you can look across the distance without wanting to close it up, if you can own your longing in the same way that you own the beauty of that blue that can never be possessed? For something of this longing will, like the blue of distance, only be relocated, not assuaged, by acquisition and arrival, just as the mountains cease to be blue when you arrive among them and the blue instead tints the next beyond. Somewhere in this is the mystery of why tragedies are more beautiful than comedies and why we take a huge pleasure in the sadness of certain songs and stories. Something is always far away.

The mystic Simone Weil wrote to a friend on another continent, "Let us love this distance, which is thoroughly woven with friendship, since those who do not love each other are not separated." For Weil, love is the atmosphere that fills and colors the distance between herself and her friend. Even when that friend arrives on the doorstep, something remains impossibly remote: when you step forward to embrace them your arms are wrapped around mystery, around the unknowable, around that which cannot be possessed. The far seeps in even to the nearest. After all we hardly know our own depths.

In the fifteenth century, European painters began to paint the blue of distance. Earlier artists had not been much concerned with the faraway in their art. Sometimes a solid wall of gold backed up the saints and patrons; sometimes the space curved around as though the earth were indeed a sphere but we were on its inside. Painters became more concerned with verisimilitude, with a rendition of the world as it appeared to the human eye, and in those days when the art of perspective was just arriving, they seized upon the blue of distance as another means of giving depth and dimension to their work. Often the band of blue toward the horizon seems exaggerated: it extends too far forward, it is too abrupt a change in color, it is too blue, as though they were exulting in the phenomenon by overdoing it. Below the sky, above the putative subject of the painting, in the spaces before the horizon, they would paint a small blue world—blue sheep, blue shepherd, blue houses, blue hills, blue road, and blue cart.

You see it again and again, the blue expanse that begins at the level of Christ crucified in Solario's 1503 painting; that extends beyond the ruins before which a beautiful Virgin admires her sleeping son, laid in a robe of brighter blue, in a painting from the studio of Raphael; see it in Niccolo Dell'Abate's painting of 1571 showing a blue town and blue sky behind a classical grouping of what looks like Graces incongruously, nonchalantly pulling Moses from some rushes in a lush river whose color seems to come from the background, like leaching dye. It's there in both Italian and northern paintings. In Hans Memling's triptych of the Resurrection circa 1490, the toes and robe hem of a levitating figure are ascending out of the frame, daringly cropped like a figure in a photograph, though there are no photographs of miracles. Below, a group of brown-haired figures looks upward, their hands raised in prayer and astonishment. Just above their heads is the near shore of a lake. The lake is blue and beyond it are blue hills, as though there were three realms, the heaven whose sunset colors the floating figure is entering, the many-colored earth below, and the faraway blue realm that is neither, not part of this Christian duality. The effect is even more pronounced in Joachim Patenier's famous painting of Saint Jerome in the wilderness, made about thirty years later. Jerome crouches in a ragged-roofed hovel before a pile of deep gray rocks, and behind him much of the world is blue, blue river, blue rocks, blue hills, as though he were in exile not from civilization, but from this particular celestial shade. However, like one of the figures in Memling's painting, Jerome is clad in a soft blue, as are so many Virgin Marys, as though they were clad in the faraway, as though some part of this ambiguous faraway had moved forward.

In his 1474 portrait of Ginevra de'Benci, Leonardo painted just a narrow band of blue trees and blue horizon at the back, behind the brownish trees that frame the pale stern woman whose bodice laces up with a lace the same blue, but he loved atmospheric effects. He wrote that when painting buildings, "to make one appear more distant than another, you should represent the air as rather dense. Therefore make the first building . . . of its own color; the next most distant make less outlined and more blue; that which you wish to show at yet another distance, make bluer yet again; and that which is five times more distant make five times more blue." The painters seemed to have become smitten with the blue of distance, and when you look at these paintings you can imagine a world where you could walk through an expanse of green grass, brown tree trunks, of whitewashed houses, and then at some point arrive in the blue country: grass, trees, houses become blue, and perhaps if you look down at yourself, you too would be blue as the Hindu god Krishna.

This world was realized in the cyanotypes, or blue photographs, of the nineteenth century—*cyan* means blue, though I always thought the term referred to the cyanide with which the prints were made. Cyanotypes were cheap and easy to make, and so some amateurs chose to work in cyanotype altogether, some professional photographers used the medium to make preliminary prints, treated so that they would fade and vanish in a few weeks' time: these vanishing prints were made as samples from which to order permanent images in other tones. In the cyanotypes you arrive in this world where darkness and light are blue and white, where bridges and people and apples are blue as lakes, as though everything were seen through the melancholy atmosphere that here is cyanide. The color persisted in postcards through the middle of the twentieth century: I own some of blue palaces and blue glaciers, blue monuments and blue train stations.

There is an album of oval photographs made sometime in the late nineteenth century by a man named Henry Bosse. All the pictures are of the upper Mississippi River, and they are all cyanotype blue. At first, they seem to portray an enchanted realm, the river once upon a time, but Bosse was working with the engineers who were strangling and straightening the river, turning it from a meandering wild thing with islands and eddies and marshy edges into something narrower and faster-flowing, a dredged, banked stream for the rapid flow of commerce. They made wing dams, outcroppings that trapped sediment and erased the natural edges of the river, dredged it and locked it, but Bosse's pictures are more beautiful than documentation and engineering require, each one a cameo of blue, blue all the way to the foreground of blue railroad yards and blue bridges under construction. But in this world we actually live in, distance ceases to be distance and to be blue when we arrive in it. The far becomes the near, and they are not the same place.

One year of drought the Great Salt Lake fell so low that much of what was ordinarily sea became land, and I went out walking on it toward Antelope Island, which floated above its reflection, a symmetrical solid object like a precious stone, floating in that blue. Miles and miles of what had not long ago been lake had become a puzzle-patchwork of shallow pools and damp and dry sand, shallow lagoons of clear water, long fingers of sand that stretched toward the island and its reflection in the deeper blue water beyond. Sometimes the sandbars ended in water and I had to find another way forward, but I could more or less walk directly toward the island for the miles and hours I was out. I walked across ground that was sometimes ribbed sand, sometimes smooth, that sometimes caved in underfoot, as though there were pockets of air underneath, that sometimes squelched so that my footprints were surrounded by paler sand where the water had been pressed away by my weight. With that long line of foot-prints unfurling behind me, I couldn't get literally lost but I lost track of time, becoming lost in that other way that isn't about dislocation but about the immersion where everything else falls away.

Sometimes there were small sprays of brown oak leaves on the ground, though there were no trees any-where within sight and shore was far away. Sometimes sodden crumpled clots of feather and bone that had once been birds sat on the strand. How the leaves ar-rived, how the birds died, was unfathomable, that word meaning depths that cannot be plumbed. Behind me etched high into the rocks and mountains beyond the Great Salt Lake was the waterline of Lake Bon-neville, which had been so much bigger, so much deeper, long ago in a wetter era on earth, when red-woods grew in Arizona and Death Valley was likewise a lake. Ten thousand years or more have passed since that lake ceased to exist, but its ring all around the landscape insisted that where I walked was once deep underwater, just as the flotsam and soft sand reminded me that not so long ago I could have rowed or swum where I was walking. This was new land, temporary land, that would be drowned in winter, and years might pass before it would be walkable again, or cen-turies. Antelope Island, golden in the harsh light, would get larger and clearer as I walked but always re-main ahead like a dream or a hope. The water that re-mained was pale blue and on that scorching October

||||||

afternoon a pale sky met it far away, the distinction between water and air hard to make out.

Lost in the walking that set me loose in the moorings
of time, I thought of the talk I had given in Salt Lake
City. To try to describe the profundity of change we fail
to register, I had told a story from another lake, from
Lake Titicaca in Bolivia. When I was two, we lived in
Lima, Peru, for a year, and all of us, mother, father,
brothers, and I, went up into the Andes once, and then
sailed across Lake Titicaca, from Peru to Bolivia. Lake
Titicaca, one of those high-altitude lakes, Tahoe, Como,
Constance, Atitlán, like blue eyes staring back at the
blue sky.

One day a few years ago my mother took out of her
cedar chest the turquoise blouse she bought for me on
that trip to Bolivia, a miniature of the native women's
outfits. When she unfolded the little garment and gave
it to me, the living memory of wearing the garment
collided shockingly with the fact that it was so tiny,
with arms less than a foot long, with a tiny bodice for a
small cricket cage of a ribcage that was no longer mine,
and the shock was that my vivid memory included
what it felt like to be inside that brocade shirt but not
the fact that inside it I had been so diminutive, had
been something utterly other than my adult self who
remembered. The continuity of memory did not measure the abyss between a toddler's body and a woman's.

When I recovered the blouse, I lost the memory, for
the two were irreconcilable. It vanished in an instant,

and I saw it go. Sometimes you hear of murals and miraculously preserved bodies buried, sealed, protected from light for hundreds or thousands of years. Exposed to the fresh air and light for the first time, they begin to fade, crumble, disappear. Sometimes gaining and losing are more intimately related than we like to think. And some things cannot be moved or owned. Some light does not make it all the way through the atmosphere, but scatters.

I put the blouse away in my own trunk and then took it out when I began to think of it again and found that my memory had turned it into something more familiar, into the velvet blouses Navajo women and girls wear. The Bolivian blouse was beaded, and it had a zigzag neckline of soft blue piping and two blue bows whose ribbons were pressed into flat creases long ago, but the fabric was a striped brocade. It was turquoise, the blue of swimming pools and of semiprecious stones, brighter than the sky. Bolivia, I said to a friend, who heard, Oblivion.

When I first began to write, I had been a child for most of my life, and my childhood memories were vivid and potent, the forces that shaped me. Most of them have grown fainter with time, and whenever I write one down, I give it away: it ceases to have the shadowy life of memory and becomes fixed in letters; it ceases to be mine; it loses that mobile unreliability of the live, just as the blouse ceased to be something I recalled being inside and became the garment worn by that unrecognizable toddler in the snapshot when it was handed to me. A person in her twenties has been a child for most of her life, but as time goes by that portion that is childhood becomes smaller and smaller, more and more distant, more and more faded, though they say at the end of life the beginning returns with renewed vividness, as though you had sailed all the way around the world and were going back into the darkness from which you came. For the elderly, often the nearby and recent become vague and only the faraway in time and space is vivid.

For children, it's the distance that holds little interest. Gary Paul Nabhan writes about taking his children to the Grand Canyon, where he realized "how much time adults spend scanning the landscape for picturesque panoramas and scenic overlooks. While the kids were on their hands and knees, engaged with what was immediately before them, we adults traveled by abstraction." He adds that whenever they approached a promontory, his son and daughter would "abruptly release their hands from mine, to scour the ground for bones, pine cones, sparkly sandstone, feathers, or wildflowers." There is no distance in childhood: for a baby, a mother in the other room is gone forever, for a child the time until a birthday is endless. Whatever is absent is impossible, irretrievable, unreachable. Their mental landscape is like that of medieval paintings: a foreground full of vivid things and then a wall. The blue of distance comes with time, with the discovery of melancholy, of loss, the texture of longing, of the complexity of the terrain we traverse, and with the years of travel.

If sorrow and beauty are all tied up together, then perhaps maturity brings with it not what Nabhan calls abstraction, but an aesthetic sense that partially redeems the losses time brings and finds beauty in the faraway.

Antelope Island grew closer and closer, larger and clearer, but finally there was a point at which there was no going on. Or perhaps there was but it would have meant swimming in that sea that even in its usual state is far saltier than the ocean and in this drought must have been intensely concentrated. I can imagine another version of that journey in which I stripped and swam, burning my back and bobbing like a cork, to the island, but I do not know what I would have done upon arrival. And I'm not sure the island was meant to be arrived at, for up close its glowing gold would have dissolved into scrub and soil.

When I had gone as far as I could walk, I looked down and the scalloped edges of land and water lost scale and looked like the world seen from an airplane. Airplane flights are usually from city to city, but in between are the untrodden realms to which you can only give approximate labels—somewhere in Newfoundland, somewhere in Nebraska or the Dakotas. From miles up in the sky, the land looks like a map of itself, but without any of the points of reference that make maps make sense. The oxbows and mesas out the window are anonymous, unfathomable, a map without words. I've found out that the wish the plane would do an emergency landing in one of them is widespread among those who go from city to city on their work. These nameless places awaken a desire to be lost, to be far away, a desire for that melancholy wonder that is the blue of distance. And that day at the Great Salt Lake as I looked at my feet, even those feet seemed a great distance away, in this terrain without scale, in which the near and the far folded into each other, in which puddles were oceans and sand ridges mountain ranges.

I walked back, the island behind me and before me the ruinous Salt Palace where the truck awaited, back into the world of ordinary clutter. But near where I'd started there was one more surprise in that landscape: a series of shallow indentations where water had dried into salt crystals. One was a carpet of roses, one a heap of straws, one a field of snowflakes, all made of muddy salt, though when I tried to cut away a small cluster of the pale brown roses to take with me, they immediately became less beautiful. Some things we have only as long as they remain lost, some things are not lost only so long as they are distant.

Daisy

Chains

Things in my family have a way of disappearing. When I was much younger, my father's baby sister showed me a whole box of family photographs, and the blank wall that lay behind my own beginnings gave way under a cascade of cardboard-mounted formal poses and strange unnamed faces in all the range from sepia to gelatin-silver gray. My aunt and I sat for a long time with the cardboard box in her living room cast into almost perpetual gloom by redwood trees, turning over images while she recited names I knew and names I didn't. The photograph that made the greatest impression on me was of my grandmother and her two younger brothers at Ellis Island or from about the time they came through that great portal of immigration in New York Harbor. They were lined up in an overlapping row according to height and the conventions of the era's portrait photography. Their heads had been shaved, perhaps for lice or ringworm, and they had the hollow-eyed, haunted look of so many immigrants of the time, these three children in their matching white sailor suits who had got themselves all the way across Europe and the Atlantic and would cross another continent alone.

When I asked about the photographs long afterward, my aunt said that the box of images didn't exist and I must have imagined the whole thing. A few years later, I asked again, and she acknowledged the box's existence but said it had vanished. Photographs, which are supposed to serve as the anchors of an objective past, are as unstable as everything else that constitutes my paternal family history. My father and aunt are gone now, their parents gone long before, and there is no one to repeat or contradict the few scattered stories they told. Each story came as a surprise, an utterance not to be questioned, elicited, repeated, and they had the enigmatic brevity of oracles and newspaper filler items. In some ways this paternal family history resembles the place it came from, in which countries were devoured and regurgitated by empires, borders fluctuated in disregard of language and culture, in which communism suppressed the past with the airbrushed photograph as its famous adjunct, so that images kept pace with the times and those who disappeared from the world also disappeared from pictures of it. The three children with the shaved heads had emigrated from Bialystok, which had long ago been in Lithuania, then Poland, then Prussia, was once held by Napoleon's troops, was Russia during the time of their emigrations, a much-bombed war zone between Germany and Russia in the first world war, occupied again in the next world war by the Germans who would make the Jews disappear.

||||||

It may be too that truth was not a fixed quantity for my family, poured as it was back and forth from the various languages they spoke, just as emigration didn't constitute the same kind of displacement for people whose diaspora had begun so long before. At home they spoke neither Russian nor Polish but Yiddish, a medieval German dialect, though they weren't German either but heirs of the diaspora that had begun in Israel almost two millennia before (if not, as the blue eyes and blond hair among us testified, pure descendants). Nothing of that tongue survived into my generation but a few insults: Yiddish can describe defects of character with the precision that Inuit describes ice or Japanese rain. Another language, Hebrew, was preserved for other uses, and an indelible image of a then imaginary homeland kept those speakers from melting into their surroundings. I wonder sometimes about the merit of that miraculous tenacity, that adherence to a lost landscape and a senescent language. A case could be made that they would have been better off melting into the landscape as no doubt many now forgotten did, adopting native tongues, stories, places to love, ceasing to be exiles by ceasing to remember the country they were exiled from so that they could wholly embrace the country they were in. Only by losing that past would they lose the condition of exile, for the place they were exiled from no longer existed, and they were no longer the people who had left it. Perhaps that willful forgetting, that refusal to tell tales, came from the wish that we could become native to the New World as they never did, never could, to the Old.

Everyone who survived the Holocaust survived it because they had left behind this hostile interim homeland, and only one woman went back. She had been saved by love, her daughter told me long afterward in Los Angeles. She had fallen in love with a Russian her family urged her not to marry, followed her heart into Russia anyway, and survived there during the Second World War that took her husband when she was pregnant with her younger child, a son. After the war this widow went back to join her family in Poland, but every one of them had been exterminated. She stayed on alone with her children until tuberculosis took her when they were still small. They were consigned to an orphanage run by anti-Semitic nuns and then, when their ethnicity was discovered, shipped off to Israel. The son as far as I know lives there still, but the daughter went to France to study and later came to the United States. She had lived with bedouins in the Negev desert, with royalty in Kashmir, with architects in Arizona. On the table in her bedroom were small glasses of soil, beautiful powders in ochers and reds and even lavender she had gathered in deserts around the world, and it was as though through being uprooted so many times this was all the homeland that was left to her, this collection of earths like the jars of rouge and powder another woman might have on her vanity. Since then we have lost touch. But she was related to my grandfather, not my grandmother.

My grandmother's mother disappeared too, or so I was told. As often happened, her father left first, then sent for his wife when he had established himself in the New World, in Los Angeles, and earned passage money for her. Later, he sent for the children, who had been lodged with relatives after their parents had departed. Or that's what I was once told, when I was told that my great-grandmother disappeared somewhere between Eastern Europe and the West Coast of the United States. I used to imagine all the things that could have happened between the two places, picture her getting off a train somewhere on the prairie, getting lost and staying lost, starting up an unimaginable new life unlike the one allotted to her by her family and her ethnicity, stepping out of the noisy compression of an Isaac Bashevis Singer story into the expansive calm of a Willa Cather novel. The vast spaces of the American West, so little known to its immigrants even now, have always invited travelers to lose their past like so much luggage and reinvent themselves.

I realize now that it was my own desire to step out of the train, the car, the conversation, the obligation, into the landscape that I gave this imagined ancestor. I grew up with landscape as recourse, with the possibility of exiting the horizontal realm of social relations for a vertical alignment with earth and sky, matter and spirit. Vast open spaces speak best to this craving, the spaces I myself first found in the desert and then in the western grasslands. Such spaces are not as easy to enter as might be imagined; they are often the private land one passes on the way to the public lands of trees and steepness, private both because prizing nothingness is harder than prizing something and because when they aren't the utter blankness of desert-dry lake beds they are useful for growing or grazing.

One Independence Day a few years ago, I was at a picnic at a huge cattle ranch in northeastern New Mexico, a stranger to the people there except the friends who brought me. In this the monsoon season, the grass was a green carpet patterned with small burrows, stubby cacti, and with wildflowers from which bright insects leapt at my approach. It rolled on uninterrupted to the blue mountains a day's walk or more away, an expanse in which it seemed you'd never have to stop or would have become transformed by the time you'd traversed that whole distance. With excuses to the party I went into it, walking until the cluster of cottonwoods and elms, sole trees in all that vastness, had grown small long after the people beneath them had vanished. Summer breezes caressed me, my legs stepped forward as though possessed of their own appetites, and the mountains kept promising. I stopped before the trees were gone, not ready that day to disappear entirely into the vastness. Perhaps these spaces are the best corollary I have found to truth, to clarity, to independence.

"Emptiness is the track on which the centered person moves," said a Tibetan sage six hundred years ago, and the book where I found this edict followed it with an explanation of the word "track" in Tibetan: *shul,* "a mark that remains after that which made it has passed by—a footprint, for example. In other contexts, shul is used to describe the scarred hollow in the ground where a house once stood, the channel worn through rock where a river runs in flood, the indentation in the grass where an animal slept last night. All of these are shul: the impression of something that used to be there. A path is a shul because it is an impression in the ground left by the regular tread of feet, which has kept it clear of obstructions and maintained it for the use of others. As a shul, emptiness can be compared to the impression of something that used to be there. In this case, such an impression is formed by the indentations, hollows, marks, and scars left by the turbulence of selfish craving." In Yiddish, shul means a synagogue, but I was trying to send this missing ancestor not to temple but to a path through an uninhabited expanse where heaven seems to come all the way down to your feet.

For a long time I imagined that she was the woman in Lewis Hine's 1905 photograph "Young Russian Jewess at Ellis Island." For a photographer known for his social documentary work, it's a strange image, with its brooding, intense face and its indistinct, soft-focus background. Ellis Island, which in most photographs appears overrun by people, is empty and still here. The only indication of place is the blurry bars of the fenced walkways through which lines of people were processed in the Great Hall. This image of such a private and solitary moment in the packed bustle of Ellis Island is a document of an anomaly in the place and in the work of Hine. It's not about social conditions. It's about the soul. A woman with a scarf or shawl pushed back, just far enough to show her dark hair, parted in the middle and not recently washed, looks at something past the camera, neither intimidated nor engaged by it. Only her cloth coat with its asymmetrical closure places her as being from the far eastern fringes of Europe. Up close she is nearly beautiful, young and somehow tender, but from further away or with a smaller or darker reproduction, you can see the skull in the set face of this emigrant, as though through hunger, exhaustion, fear, she is close to other borders than national ones. Above her shadowed eye sockets, her forehead gleams as white as the sky behind her. It's as though we can see through it to the same distant pallor that is the sky, or as though both are only absences on the photographic paper.

Long after the image of the woman stepping onto the prairie was secure as a talisman, I was told that my great-grandmother didn't disappear. Her husband had her incarcerated in a mental hospital when she arrived in California, and her three children arrived to find that their father had married again, this time to an American woman, and had a new daughter. I imagined the rest, my grandmother arriving to find that she had been supplanted by a half-sister fluent in the English she would have to learn and would speak with a heavy accent the rest of her life. She seems to have found her way at first, joining according to another photograph a ladies' hiking club: stalwart young women

||||||

in knee-high lace-up boots and bloomers so uniform they look like a military group, up in the young, piney mountains of Los Angeles. I cannot pick her out of the group of olive-skinned maidens with hopeful gazes. She married my grandfather, another immigrant from a nearby town in the Russian Pale sometime in the later 1920s, brought over by his older brother after he was caught up in the throes of the Russian Revolution. They met in a Jewish hiking club, someone once mentioned, and this fact doesn't fit in with anything else about them, for they seemed utterly urban, shrunk into their bodies as tenements of flesh, not as instruments of adventure in the open space of the New World. This is the closest in fact these ancestors get to my fantasy of getting off the train in the prairie.

My great-grandmother disappeared from her children's lives. And the question is whether this woman chose to disappear or couldn't find her way out of her own thoughts. Was she lost only to them because she had found another way, or was she lost to herself as well, bereft of the ability to navigate the world and her own mind? The mind too can be imagined as a landscape, but only the minds of sages might resemble the short-grass prairie in which I played with getting lost and vanishing. The rest of us have caverns, glaciers, torrential rivers, heavy fogs, chasms that open up underfoot, even marauding wildlife bearing family names. It's a landscape in which getting lost is easy and some regions are terrifying to visit. There's a Buddhist story about a man galloping by a monk who asks, Where are you going? Ask my horse, says the man. And this un-controllable emotion doesn't let you pick your destination or even see it. It's the simplest form of madness, one most of us taste some of the time.

My grandmother appeared in my life as abruptly as her mother must have disappeared. No one mentioned I had a grandmother other than my mother's seldom-seen Irish-American parent in the East, until one day on a trip to Los Angeles not long after we moved back to California, before I started school. We drove up to a tall concrete institution in a sea of asphalt, and this unanticipated ancestor came down and kissed me while we stood outside. She left lipstick on my cheek, and my mother turned around and gave a little scream because she thought it was blood. Later on, she was transferred from this place to the state asylum in Napa, not far from where we lived. For years I thought it was a re-tirement home, because she was on a ward populated entirely by elderly women who, thirsty for the sight of children, used to flock around us and give us coins when we visited, and because no one told me other-wise. It was an uncannily tranquil place full of broad lawns scattered with trees casting pleasant shade around them. When I try to recall it now I remember the red-winged blackbirds we used to see in the marshes of San Pablo Bay on our way there; and an afternoon or many afternoons my younger brother and I spent making daisy chains on one of the lawns there, which my grandmother wore till they were wilted around her

54

||||||

A
Field
Guide
to
Getting
Lost

vast bosom and hunched back; and I remember the cherry cider stand under a huge tree we used to stop at on the way home and the taste of cherries. It never occurred to me to ask her about the past, and she probably wouldn't have had much to say.

She was supposed to be a paranoid schizophrenic. That was the diagnosis she was institutionalized with during the last decades of her life. I always thought that her worldview might have been perfectly reasonable under the circumstances, though by the time I met her she was a ruin of a human being, her mind altered by shock treatment and years of drugs and by whatever toll institutions take. It's hard to say whether it was pain or the past that was being extirpated or whether they were the same thing. The doctors who treated her were unlikely to have experienced such profound instability: disappearing mothers, the vast gap between the medieval Russian-Polish Pale and glittering amnesiac Los Angeles, the three or four languages she left behind and the English she never completely acquired, the annihilation of the world she came from and of the relatives she left behind. Post-traumatic stress disorder is an alternate diagnosis a therapist once proffered for her behavior, a condition that recognized all the kinds of war she survived and a world in which nothing was too far-fetched or terrible to be possible.

I can count on one hand the stories my father told me about his childhood and family. He was a foot taller than his parents and, with his blue eyes and once-blond hair, far, far fairer than his mother, as though he sprang directly from Southern California with all its sunlight and abundance. He was part of that great assimilationist wave of the 1950s, when the ethnic past was regarded as unnecessary baggage, when America believed in the future like a religion. It's not hard to imagine why he wanted to erase his rogue father and his crazy mother from his identity, though he was more like them than he looked, riding all kinds of runaway horses all his life. My father's younger sister, my aunt, was as dark as her mother, and in her teens, when she lived with her father in El Paso, she was routinely suspected of being a Mexican and often had trouble coming back across the Rio Grande from Juárez. From her second husband, she got the surname to go with her appearance and passed as a Latina from then on. Caustic, literary, radical, she was the keeper of the family stories and photographs, though they served less as buttresses of a stable sense of the past than phantasms and fictions that metamorphose continually in accordance with the needs of the present. But all histories and photographs do that, public as well as private.

Another time my aunt hung a picture of her mother, my grandmother, in her house, another image I saw there only once. It showed a child standing next to a rough-hewn wooden farm implement. Had photography existed five hundred years ago, it wouldn't have been hard to imagine this was a photograph from that time. It conveyed how backward was the world from which my grandmother came to the sunny optimistic boomtown of Los Angeles in the teens or twenties. The people in the photographs my aunt sometimes showed me seemed to have little or nothing to do with me; their faces, their poses, their clothes spoke more of time and place than of family and kinship. The technology and conventions of photography have given a particular look to each generation's images, while history, fashion, and food have left their impressions on each body, so that nearly everyone in a given era has a kind of kinship to each other they don't to other generations. Before the 1960s, light and air themselves seem to have had an almost undersea depth and luminosity, in which skin glowed opalescently and everything seemed to have a faint aura slaughtered by the newer black-and-white films made with less silver in the emulsion. I think most Americans who didn't live through it think the Depression took place in a world of rough-hewn but secretly seductive black-and-white surfaces, as though texture itself could be a wealth to counter all that poverty. And the early part of the last century, when light was harsh and came from high above, was full of hollow-socketed stern faces above body-belying clothes. There are fossils of seashells high in the Himalayas; what was and what is are different things.

About a decade ago, one of my brothers visited our cousins in Mexico City. These were our grandmother's first cousins with whom she had stayed after her parents had emigrated and who emigrated to Mexico around the time she came to the U.S. The patriarch of that family, who had begun as a street peddler and become a wealthy art collector, remembered their childhood together and told my brother that our great-grandmother had never reached Ellis Island and the U.S. at all, but had been put in an asylum in Russia. When I heard that story, the image of the young Russian Jewess at Ellis Island suddenly vanished from my imaginary family album and became an impersonal image, a Lewis Hine image from the world called documentary, and the nameless woman from whom I'm descended became faceless and unimaginable again. I wonder now about what I was looking for when I seized upon stories and images to fill the void of her unknowability. That picture of Hine's was taken in 1905, the year my grandmother was born, before her brothers were born, too soon to be my ancestor who likely never even reached Ellis Island. Though my aunt's unreliability was visible then, my own is visible now: I can see that Hine's picture looked a little like a dark haunted version of me and not at all like my grandmother, though who knows what, in the lottery of qualities that made up my father's family of tall short pale dark people, her mother looked like.

I think sometimes that I became a historian because I didn't have a history, but also because I was interested in telling the truth in a family in which truth was an elusive entity. It could be best served not by claiming an authoritative and disinterested relationship to the facts, but by disclosing your own desires and agendas, for truth lies not only in incidents but in hopes and needs. The histories I've written have often been hidden, lost, neglected, too broad or too amorphous to show up in others' radar screens, histories that are not neat fields that belong to someone but the paths and waterways that meander through many fields and belong to no one. Art history in particular is often cast as an almost biblical lineage, a long line of begats in which painters descend purely from painters. Just as the purely patrilineal Old Testament genealogies leave out the mothers and even the fathers of the mothers, so these tidy stories leave out all the sources and inspirations that come from other media and other encounters, from poems, dreams, politics, doubts, a childhood experience, a sense of place, leave out the fact that history is made more of crossroads, branchings, and tangles than straight lines. These other sources I called the grandmothers.

But this great-grandmother of mine represents something else. To have such an immediate ancestor who represented mystery and the unknown might perhaps be a gift, generous as the empty air above the prairie is generous, just as some questions are more profound than their answers. Shul, the path that is the impression of what used to be there, is what she is now, is perhaps the route I'm traveling. I could check genealogies and track down distant relations and find out the true story. But that is her true story, and mine is that I grew up with these shifting stories. And now, so many years after I first pictured a woman stepping onto a prairie, what seems vivid and near are the red-winged blackbirds on the marsh on the way to the mental hospital and the cherry cider on the way home, its taste like the red flash of the birds flying among the cattails. Often when I see the daisies the size of nickels and dimes that grow on lawns around here, I think of those wilting daisy chains. It is as though the birds were my kin, the place my ancestors, cherry juice the blood in my veins.

My aunt has nothing more to say on the subject. We spent her last day on earth together. A friend of hers had called me the evening before to say that her lung cancer was rapidly getting worse, though we still thought she had a month or so left then. I was busier than I'd ever been before, and it was out of character for me to drop my work so quickly, but for some reason I drove up the next morning to the forest in which she lived. Her house was on the north slope of what had been a Victorian summer resort, a place never meant to be inhabited year-round even before the redwoods grew back and brought with them permanent shade and damp. Her clammy house made her illness worse, as did her five cats, but she was determined to stay home until the end. Her proudest accomplishment had been a precedent-setting lawsuit twenty years before to defend this community's watershed against logging.

So I traveled north past the town I grew up in and past more towns and apple orchards and vineyards into the somber redwoods and up the steep short dirt roads to her house. She was wasting away, and her eyes were wide and frightened. She breathed pure oxygen from a softly hissing apparatus. The cats walked across the table strewn with books and magazines. I gave her my first copy of my new book and convinced her to leave the house with her portable oxygen tank. We had planned to go out to lunch to celebrate my victories, which I always tried to insist were hers too, since she had supplied me with books and examples long before I began to write. She directed me to drive a way I hadn't driven before as she spoke of many things, of how much she loved this place, of how she regretted that she wouldn't live to see me buy land, of her children, of my family, this other branch of a small tree, of my future. Afterward, it seemed that day we had said everything that needed to be said.

The river we had been following flowed into the sea, becoming broad and tranquil at its mouth, and the afternoon light lit it to silver, the same silver as the sea. I looked and two things that had been stories seemed fact at that moment: the belief of many coastal tribes that the souls of the dead go west over the sea, and the description of death as the point at which the river enters the sea. I had driven my aunt to her death, or as it seemed in that luminousness, still like the moment after a peal of thunder, both of us to meet death. The forest we had come from seemed darker in this cool blaze of water and light, and we had entered the colorless, radiant landscape of death, charged with something as vital as life, too majestic to be terrifying, transfigured into another world. It was a little farther to the restaurant where we sat so that I saw her and she saw that ocean. The next day she sank into delirium, and she died at home four days after that trip to the sea.

Nine months later the two photographs I had remembered so vividly showed up at my cousin's house in Scotland (two of my aunt's three children have returned to Europe, as though the transplant to new soil didn't take for them; their mother excoriated the United States in classic leftist style, but she loved her redwood forest, her river, her house, and rarely went far from them). Looking at those photographs I realized how much they had changed in my imagination. And only as I sit down to write this do I realize that I too have erased the past. I always knew that my middle name was an anglicized version of a great-grandmother's name, but I dropped it in my teens, not liking its sound and feeling that a middle name was unnecessary, given how few people have my last name. Only now have I realized which great-grandmother that name belonged to, only writing this story do I know the name of that unknown woman and that it is also mine, or is now the blank space between my names.

62

The

Blue

of

Distance

In 1527 the Spaniard Álvar Núñez Cabeza de Vaca refused his commander's orders to take the ships of their expedition to a safe port while the commander and most of the men marched inland to explore. Narváez, the commander, asked why, and Cabeza de Vaca, the expedition's second in command, answered "that I felt certain he would never find the ships again, or they him, as anyone could predict from the woefully inadequate preparation; that I would rather hazard the danger that lay ahead in the interior than give any occasion for questioning my honor by remaining safely aboard." So the incompetent Narváez, Cabeza de Vaca, and three hundred men traveled north for fifteen days among the dwarf fan palms of an uninhabited expanse of what Juan Ponce de León had named Florida fourteen years before. They had met natives who told them that to the north was "a province called Apalachen, where was much gold and plenty of everything we wanted." Honor and greed would be the two gates through which Cabeza de Vaca entered the realm of the utter unknown.

The Apalachen they found was a village of forty thatched houses with ripe corn in the fields, dry corn in storage, deerskins, and "small, poor quality shawls" as all its treasure. The gold seekers marched onward, wading through lakes, tramping for days, skirmishing with natives, eating their horses, building barges to head toward Mexico and the Spanish settlements there, not knowing how far away they were, dying of armor-piercing arrows, of disease, of hunger, of drowning. No one will ever be lost like those early conquistadors again, wandering a continent about which they knew nothing, not its topography, its climate, encountering inhabitants with whom there was no common language, plunging into a place for which they had no words for places, for plants, for the animals—skunks, alligators, bison—so unlike those of their own continent.

Eduardo Galeano notes that America was conquered, but not discovered, that the men who arrived with a religion to impose and dreams of gold never really knew where they were, and that this discovery is still taking place in our time. This suggests that most European-Americans remained lost over the centuries, lost not in practical terms but in the more profound sense of apprehending where they truly were, of caring what the history of the place was and its nature. Instead, they named it after the places they had left and tried to reconstruct those places through imported plants, animals, and practices, though pumpkin, maple, and other staples would enter their diet as words like Connecticut and Dakota and raccoon would enter their vocabularies. But Cabeza de Vaca and his companions would be conquered by this land and its people, and he at least seems to have found out where he was. All but four of the six hundred men who set out on the expedition died in this place they did not know, either quickly, of violence, illness, or hunger, or slowly, as slaves or adopted members of tribes, and their stories are mostly lost to history.

At the Mississippi Delta, Narváez put the strongest and healthiest men on his barge and rowed ahead, abandoning the two other barges. Days passed. One barge was lost in a storm. Cabeza de Vaca commanded the other, whose men had all "fallen over on one another, close to death. Few were any longer conscious. Not five could stand. When night fell, only the navigator and I remained able to tend the barge. Two hours after dark, he told me I must take over; he believed he was going to die that night." After midnight, Cabeza de Vaca recalls, "I would have welcomed death rather than see so many around me in such a condition." At dawn, he heard breakers; at daylight, they found the land that was probably Galveston Island in Texas; and the men "began to recover their senses, their locomotion, and their hope." Natives fed them fish and roots; they embarked again but the barge capsized near shore; and "the survivors escaped as naked as they were born, with the loss of everything we had." They fell upon the mercy of the natives again. Winter had come, the Spaniards commenced to starve, the natives began to die of the dysentery that came with them, and the sixteen survivors of the ninety or so shipwrecked named the place the Island of Doom.

Cabeza de Vaca became a slave to this tribe, leading an "unbearable" life of hard work, including digging roots out of water and out of canebrakes. He was pared back to nothing, no language, no clothes, no weapons, no power, but he escaped and established a career as a trader of seashells, red ocher, and mesquite beans in the region. He seems to have had remarkable physical stamina and an ability to reinvent himself again and again. He walked for days and weeks on one austere meal a day. He became a slave again. He met up with some fellow survivors and with them escaped this new captivity. They arrived in the territory of another indigenous nation where they were welcomed as healers and stayed until spring. And what is remarkable about this point in his narrative is that he reports that he got lost looking for mesquite bean pods. He had so adapted to this new life he had fallen into that he no longer considered himself lost until he lost track of the route and his companions in the pathless region of the mesquites. He traveled for five days, carrying burning brands so he could keep himself warm with fires at night, and on the fifth he caught up with his fellow survivors from the Narváez expedition and with the Indians, who fed him prickly pears.

Because they went naked in the scorching sun, he reports, he and his companions "shed our skins twice a year like snakes" and suffered sores from sun, wind, and chafing labor (though one of them, Estevanico or Esteban, "the negro," was from Africa and must have fared better when it came to burning). And again "we became physicians, of whom I was the boldest and most venturous in trying to cure anything. Confidence in our ministrations as infallible extended to a belief that none could die while we were among them." Months passed among various tribes, years had passed since the disasters in Florida. They continued to travel west. Somewhere along the way they seem to have become sacred beings, these naked, relentless survivors whose journey had became a triumphal procession accompanied by three or four thousand locals. Each new village greeted them as miracle workers, holding dances in their honor. They received copper rattles, coral beads, turquoises, five green arrowheads whose malachite Cabeza de Vaca took for emerald, and an offering of six hundred deer hearts. They had been wandering for nine years by the time they arrived in what he called the Village of Hearts.

Soon after, they found evidence and heard news of conquistadors: they had arrived in what is now New Mexico, a "vast territory, which we found vacant, the inhabitants having fled to the mountains in fear of Christians." Assuring the natives that they were going to "order them to stop killing, enslaving, and dispossessing the Indians," Cabeza de Vaca and his three companions pressed on. In the report he would write afterward, Cabeza de Vaca advised that only kindness would win these people to Spanish subjection and to Christianity. One day he set out with his black-skinned companion and eleven natives, walking more than thirty miles. The following morning they caught up with slave-hunting Spaniards on horseback, who were stunned by this naked figure at ease among the people and places of this other continent. Although he had been striving for nearly a decade to return to his own people, the initial meeting was not easy. The Spaniards they met wanted to enslave Cabeza de Vaca's entourage, and he and his fellow survivors "became so angry that we went off forgetting the many Turkish-shaped bows, the many pouches, and the five emerald arrowheads, etc., which we thus lost." The Indians among whom they retreated refused to believe they were of the same tribe as the conquistadors, because "we came from the sunrise; they from the sunset; we healed the sick, they killed the sound; we came naked and barefoot, they clothed, horsed, and lanced; we coveted nothing but gave whatever we were given, while they robbed whomever they found and bestowed nothing on anyone." These men who came from the sunset were what he had been when he landed in Florida.

It took some time after he arrived in a Spanish town in Mexico before he could stand to wear clothes or sleep anywhere but on the floor. He had gone about naked, shed his skin like a snake, had lost his greed, his fear, been stripped of almost everything a human being could lose and live, but he had learned several languages, he had become a healer, he had come to admire and identify with the Native nations among whom he lived; he was not who he had been. The language of his report to the king is terse, impersonal; his declarative sentences describe only the tangibles of places, foods, encounters, and even these are given in the starkest terms, with little description, little detail. The terms in which to describe the extraordinary metamorphosis of his soul did not exist, at least for him. He was among the first, and the first to come back and tell the tale, of Europeans lost in the Americas, and like many of them he ceased to be lost not by returning but by turning into something else.

Cabeza de Vaca and his companions plunged into the American landscape, but in the centuries afterward many entered it involuntarily, as captives. Some of those who returned wrote or dictated accounts of their experiences, and these became a distinctly American genre of literature, the captivity narrative. Of course the stories of those who did not return remained unrecorded; their journeys were out of writing, out of English, into another terrain of story.

Often, initially, these strays and captives felt that they were far from home, distant from their desires, and then at some point, in a stunning reversal, they came to be at home and what they had longed for became remote, alien, unwanted. For some, perhaps there was a moment when they realized that the old longings had become little more than habit and that they were not yearning to go home but had been home for some time; for others the dreams of home must have faded by stages among the increasingly familiar details of their surroundings. They must have learned their surroundings like a language and one day woken up fluent in them. Somehow, for these castaways the far became near and the near far. They did not reject the unfamiliar but embraced it, in the course of which it became familiar. By the end of his decade of wandering, Cabeza de Vaca was no longer in harmony with his own culture, but he had kept it as a destination, a goal, that kept him purposeful and moving, even though arrival was another trauma. Many others refused to return.

In the midst of winter, in the frontier town of Deerfield, Massachusetts, 1704, Eunice Williams, age seven, was captured by a party of French and Indian raiders, along with all the other members of her family and many of their neighbors, 112 in all. They were given moccasins to wear and marched from northern Massachusetts to near Montreal through New Hampshire, in the snow. Some of the captors were wounded and dying, and some of the captives who could not keep up—notably infants, women who had recently given birth, including Williams's mother—were killed, their bodies left in the snow along the route. Many children were carried some or all of the way. Some of these child captives were not just prisoners but potential adoptees; Eunice's older brother Stephen Williams was taken by the Abenaki and then by a Pennacook chief, though he was "redeemed" as the religiously loaded term went, or ransomed, in the spring of 1705. Eunice was kept by the Mohawk Iroquois near Montreal, and she never returned.

The Iroquois practiced a ceremonious form of adoption in which a captive could replace a family member

who had died, and sometimes captives were explicit re-
placements for those killed in battle. The captive was
given a new name and treated as a member of the
family. Sometimes the given name belonged to someone who had died, and the newly named person inherited something of the affections and identity of the
deceased. Ceremoniously, officially, Eunice Williams became someone else. Within a few years, all her surviving
family members had returned to their Puritan communities, but the people among whom she lived said they
would "as soon part with their hearts" as with her. She
remained, soon forgot how to speak English, had a new
name, then a Catholic baptismal name (becoming
Catholic was almost more shocking to her Puritan
preacher father than becoming Indian), eventually a
second Iroquois name.

In 1713 in her late teens she married a member of
the community named François Xavier Arosen with
whom she remained until his death fifty-two years
later. Her brother Stephen would write in his diary in
1722 that he had seen a man come from Canada. "He
brings bad news thence. My poor sister lives with her
Indian husband; has had two children, one is living, the
other not." The Williams family never ceased to mourn
her loss and to regard her as spiritually lost as well. But
Eunice Williams had ceased to be a captive long ago.
She finally met with Stephen and her other brothers in
1740, traveled with them to their home, and even attended "publick worship" with them. "Yet this might
be as a pledge yt she may return to the house and ordi-

nances of God from wch she has been so long Sepratd," though according to tradition she refused to "put off her Indian blankets" and camped out in a meadow with her husband rather than residing in a relative's home. She was negotiating her emotional and cultural distance carefully, on her terms rather than theirs. On a few further occasions, she revisited her birth family, but she never left the community that had captured her, and in it she died at age ninety-five.

Her family always spoke as though she had crossed over into another world beyond reach, but what is striking is that even in the eighteenth century the boundaries were blurred. The Mohawks among whom she lived had close ties to the Jesuits of Montreal, and there was considerable movement between the various French, English, and Native communities. But it was different enough. She no longer spoke the language of her blood relatives, did not see them for more than three decades, and had settled among a people whose every belief and practice was profoundly different from the Puritans'. John Demos, in his book on Williams, *The Unredeemed Captive,* suggests that the Iroquois were kinder to children, and perhaps the thing hardest for whites to accept or, often, even to imagine is that some captives preferred native culture. Looking back, the cultures of Cabeza de Vaca's Spaniards and Eunice Williams's family look more forbidding, if no less remote, than the indigenous cultures among which they came to live. There is something obdurate, obsessive, inflexible about them, as hard and

||||||

angular as conquistadors' armor, as dreary as Puritan theology.

Some of this is evident in Stephen Williams's refusal to regard her as anything other than a tragedy, a captive, a person waiting to return, to understand that she had become someone else. The word *lost* in this context has many shades. The captive is at first literally lost, taken into terra incognita. And unless that captive is redeemed, he or more frequently she remains lost to the people who were left behind, and thus the language of lostness is often used to describe the person as lost the way that a possession is lost—a lost umbrella, lost keys—without recognizing that he or more commonly she may well have ceased either to be a captive or to be lost. But the word *lost* has spiritual implications, as in the line of the penitent slave trader's hymn "I once was lost but now am found"; the person taken among the heathen was commonly imagined to be spiritually lost, estranged from Christianity and civilization. Thus, whatever the condition of the former captives, they were forever imagined as lost. But they did not always imagine themselves that way, and it seems that the captives had in a sense to lose their past to join the present, and this abandonment of memory, of old ties, is the steep cost of adaptation.

Mary Jemison, who was captured with her family in Pennsylvania in 1758, told her story to a scribe, and so her voice survives as Williams's does not. There was a raid on her parents' frontier farm when she was about fifteen. An Indian followed them with a lash, forcing the children to maintain the pace. They were marched, kept without food and water for days, and then taken to "the border of a dark and dismal swamp." There she and a little boy were given moccasins, signs that their journey would continue, while the other captives, including her parents and siblings, were killed "and mangled in the most shocking manner." Like Eunice Williams, she was adopted. She was to replace a brother who had died, and the two Seneca women— "kind good natured women; peaceable and mild in their dispositions"—to whom she was given she referred to as sisters ever after. The trauma of captivity, of the murder of family members, and a sudden new life among another culture and another language must have been considerable, but adapting to it all was a matter of survival, and these child captives survived and then flourished in their new lives. The rupture must have been as sudden and violent as birth.

More than a year later, the Senecas among whom she lived brought her along on a visit to Fort Pitt (the future Pittsburgh), where the whites took such an interest in her that her sisters "hurried me into their canoe and recrossed the river" and rowed the long journey home without stopping. "The sight of white people who could speak English inspired me with an unspeakable anxiety to go home with them, and share in the blessings of civilization. My sudden departure and escape from them, seemed like a second captivity, and for a long time I brooded the thought of my miserable situation with almost as much sorrow and dejection as

I had done those of my first sufferings. Time, the destroyer of every affection, wore away my unpleasant feelings, and I became as contented as before. We tended our cornfields through the summer...." She married, she bore a child, she lost a husband, and by that time she was at home among the Seneca.

Once again the possibility of returning to the white community appeared when a Dutchman began stalking her in hope of capturing her and turning her in for a bounty. Jemison chose not to be captured again and ran "with all the speed I was mistress of" to a hiding place. Inspired by the Dutchman, a Seneca leader thought of turning her in for the bounty himself, and she went and hid again in the weeds with her young son. She was desperate to remain where she had once yearned to leave. She remarried, bore six more children, and came to own a vast expanse of land, "by virtue of a deed from the Chiefs of the Six Nations," on which she lived the rest of her long life. That life she called, in her autobiography filtered through the pen of a scribe, "a tragical medley that I hope will never be repeated." But it was the deaths and discord of her children of which she spoke; her troubles had all become personal, and the land she lived on was itself a meeting ground between the two cultures, for she leased out land to white farmers.

For these eastern captives, the boundaries between cultures began to blur as the geographies overlapped. For Cynthia Ann Parker, there was no such blurring. In 1836, when she was nine, she and her family were captured by Comanches on the Texas plains where they had recently settled (or invaded). The rest of her family was massacred. She alone survived, married a prominent member of her new community, Peta Nocona, and bore two sons and a daughter. A quarter century later there was another battle, this time initiated by white men, and she was captured on horseback with her youngest child in arms. She was led to believe that her husband had died in the battle, but it appears that this was a mistake. Even so she never saw her husband or sons again. An uncle in Fort Worth claimed her and kept her captive, locked up at night lest she flee with her daughter. She never relearned English properly during the decade she lived among the culture that had once been and was no longer hers. A man who met her recollected that she "had a wild expression and would look down when people looked at her. She could use an ax equal to a man and disliked a lazy person. She was an expert in tanning hides with the hair on them, or plaiting or knitting either ropes or whips. She thought her two boys were lost on the prairie. This dissatisfied her very much." The whites always regarded her as having been rescued, but she seems to have regarded herself as having been imprisoned. The daughter died and ten years after her capture, Parker, who had starved herself into weakness, died of the flu. She never saw her sons again, though one came to claim her remains forty years after her death and rebury her in his world.

There are less dire stories, such as that of Thomas Jefferson Mayfield, whose family moved from Texas to California in the 1840s. They settled in the San Joaquin Valley, where their indigenous neighbors kept them stocked with fish, game, and acorn bread. When his mother died, his father, feeling unable to care for the boy while keeping up his roving business, allowed him to go off with the Choinumne Yokuts. After all the captivity narratives in which contact begins as masculine battle and after Cabeza de Vaca's violent plunge into the unknown, it's the mildness of Mayfield's transition from one culture to another that's startling. The Yokuts were maternal substitutes, though no single woman adopted him: they all looked after him, and he seems to have run in a pack of children. For a decade, his home was with them, and for periods of as long as three years he didn't see his father. Eventually, as the Civil War broke out and the Yokuts were increasingly hemmed in by white settlers, he shifted back to the culture he was born in. His memoir in some ways marks the end of the captivity narrative (though there would be other captives later in the nineteenth century), because the indigenous nations were ceasing to be free in their own land; they themselves were becoming captives within the spreading dominant culture, and few found as amiable a reception as these children did. It was no longer individuals but whole cultures being brought up abruptly into collision with difference, traversing that distance between the near and the far.

Reading these stories, it's tempting to think that the arts to be learned are those of tracking, hunting, navigating, skills of survival and escape. Even in the everyday world of the present, an anxiety to survive manifests itself in cars and clothes for far more rugged occasions than those at hand, as though to express some sense of the toughness of things and of readiness to face them. But the real difficulties, the real arts of survival, seem to lie in more subtle realms. There, what's called for is a kind of resilience of the psyche, a readiness to deal with what comes next. These captives lay out in a stark and dramatic way what goes on in every life: the transitions whereby you cease to be who you were. Seldom is it as dramatic, but nevertheless, something of this journey between the near and the far goes on in every life. Sometimes an old photograph, an old friend, an old letter will remind you that you are not who you once were, for the person who dwelt among them, valued this, chose that, wrote thus, no longer exists. Without noticing it you have traversed a great distance; the strange has become familiar and the familiar if not strange at least awkward or uncomfortable, an outgrown garment. And some people travel far more than others. There are those who receive as birthright an adequate or at least unquestioned sense of self and those who set out to reinvent themselves, for survival or for satisfaction, and travel far. Some people inherit values and practices as a house they inhabit; some of us have to burn down that house, find our own ground, build from scratch, even as a psychological metamorphosis.

||||||

As a cultural metamorphosis the transition is far more dramatic.

The people thrown into other cultures go through something of the anguish of the butterfly, whose body must disintegrate and reform more than once in its life cycle. In her novel *Regeneration,* Pat Barker writes of a doctor who "knew only too well how often the early stages of change or cure may mimic deterioration. Cut a chrysalis open, and you will find a rotting caterpillar. What you will never find is that mythical creature, half caterpillar, half butterfly, a fit emblem of the human soul, for those whose cast of mind leads them to seek such emblems. No, the process of transformation consists almost entirely of decay." But the butterfly is so fit an emblem of the human soul that its name in Greek is *psyche,* the word for soul. We have not much language to appreciate this phase of decay, this withdrawal, this era of ending that must precede beginning. Nor of the violence of the metamorphosis, which is often spoken of as though it were as graceful as a flower blooming.

I write this and then one day, with a free hour in between a conversation and an obligation, go to the old Conservatory of Flowers near my home, recently restored and reopened. I had not been there in nine years, since it was ravaged by a great winter storm. I thought I would look at the gleaming dark leaves large as maps, at the vines and mosses and orchids, and breathe that humid air, the steamy glories I remembered. But the west wing of the great greenhouse with its milky windowpanes had become a butterfly garden and in the middle of that chamber was a butterfly hatchery, a window a few inches in front of a wooden plank, or rather shallow series of shelves, to which were pinned platoons of future butterflies, sorted by species. The chrysalises had taken on the shape of the butterflies inside, and some rocked as though stirred by a faint breeze, though the adjacent chrysalises were still. Four butterflies emerged while I watched, and seven more when I returned another day.

They came out with their wings packed down like furled parachutes, like crumpled letters. Even as they emerged it seemed incredible that their wide wings had once fit in so slender a space. As they emerged, their bodies were visible as they would never quite be again, once the wings expanded and came to dominate the creature, and during those moments they looked like bugs, like insects, instead of what they would be when they were all brilliantly colored wing like some sentient cousin of flowers. Their bodies were still plump with the fluid they had to pump into those wings in the first minutes of their emergence to make them the straight sheets with which they flew. Each clung to its chrysalis while its wings unfolded by almost imperceptible stages. Some did not get quite free, and their wings never fully straightened. One butterfly sat still with an orange wing curled into the chrysalis. One seemed permanently stuck halfway out, its yellow-and-black wings like buds that would not flower. One flailed frantically, trying to drag itself out by crawling onto adjacent unopened chrysalises until they too be-

82

||||||

A
Field
Guide
to
Getting
Lost

gan to thrash, a contagious panic. That one finally dropped free, though it may have been too late for its wings to straighten. The process of transformation consists mostly of decay and then of this crisis when emergence from what came before must be total and abrupt.

But the changes in a butterfly's life are not always so dramatic. The strange resonant word *instar* describes the stage between two successive molts, for as it grows, a caterpillar, like a snake, like Cabeza de Vaca walking across the Southwest, splits its skin again and again, each stage an instar. It remains a caterpillar as it goes through these molts, but no longer one in the same skin. There are rituals marking such splits, graduations, indoctrinations, ceremonies of change, though most changes proceed without such clear and encouraging recognition. *Instar* implies something both celestial and ingrown, something heavenly and disastrous, and perhaps change is commonly like that, a buried star, oscillating between near and far.

Abandon

The most beautiful thing in the abandoned hospital was the peeling paint. The place had been painted again and again in pastels, and in the years of its abandonment these layers flaked into lozenges and curled scrolls, a different color on each side. The flakes clung to the walls like papery bark and piled up like fallen leaves. I remember walking down one long corridor illuminated only by light from distant doorways. There the paint dangled from ceiling and walls in huge wafers, and my passing stirred the air enough that some came drifting down in my wake. The movie we made there was too grainy to show such delicate details, but I remember one passage in it where I was coming down such a corridor and the shafts of light behind me were so strong on either side of my neck that my head seemed at times to detach from my body and hover above it. I had become its haunting wraith.

That was when I was twenty, half my life ago, and a boy my age made the most politely democratic proposition I ever received: would I like to make a movie with him in the ruined hospital near my San Francisco home? I would, we did, and we spent the next six years together in amazing tranquility and stayed close for a few years thereafter. He was one of those prodigies whose gifts don't show up on tests, a hardly literate mechanical-visual-spatial genius more interested in problem solving, like engineers, than in self-expression and meaning. Scripts and story lines were beyond him, so I cobbled together enough notions to let us film the hospital with his Super-Eight camera and a stock of black-and-white film he'd laid his hands on, already a rare product then. It was the early 1980s, and looking back I can see that it was a sort of golden age of ruins.

Coming of age in the heyday of punk, it was clear we were living at the end of something—of modernism, of the American dream, of the industrial economy, of a certain kind of urbanism. The evidence was all around us in the ruins of the cities. The Bronx was block after block, mile after mile of ruin, as were even some Manhattan neighborhoods, housing projects across the country were in a state of collapse, many of the shipping piers that had been key to San Francisco's and New York's economies were abandoned, as was San Francisco's big Southern Pacific rail yard and its two most visible breweries. Vacant lots like missing teeth gave a rough grin to the streets we haunted. Ruin was everywhere, for cities had been abandoned by the rich, by politics, by a vision of the future. Urban ruins were the emblematic places for this era, the places that gave punk part of its aesthetic, and like most aesthetics this one contained an ethic, a worldview with a mandate on how to act, how to live.

What is a ruin, after all? It is a human construction abandoned to nature, and one of the allures of ruins in the city is that of wilderness: a place full of the promise of the unknown with all its epiphanies and dangers. Cities are built by men (and to a lesser extent, women), but they decay by nature, from earthquakes and hurricanes to the incremental processes of rot, erosion, rust, the microbial breakdown of concrete, stone, wood, and brick, the return of plants and animals making their own complex order that further dismantles the simple order of men. This nature is allowed to take over when, for economic or political reasons, maintenance is withdrawn. Ruins are also created by the vandalism, arson, and war in which humans run wild. Cities in Europe and the American South have been consciously ruined by war, but this country's North and West have fallen into ruin only for other reasons. Ruins were the symbolic home of much of the art of the time, some photography and painting, much music, the science fiction movies of the time, even the backdrops for rock videos and fashion photographs, for clothes that looked ancient, worn, combat and cobweb stuff. They were landscapes of abandon, the abandon of neglect and violence that came first and the abandon of passion that moved into the ruins.

A city is built to resemble a conscious mind, a network that can calculate, administrate, manufacture. Ruins become the unconscious of a city, its memory, unknown, darkness, lost lands, and in this truly bring it to life. With ruins a city springs free of its plans into something as intricate as life, something that can be explored but perhaps not mapped. This is the same transmutation spoken of in fairy tales when statues and toys and animals become human, though they come to life and with ruin a city comes to death, but a generative death like the corpse that feeds flowers. An urban ruin is a place that has fallen outside the economic life of the city, and it is in some way an ideal home for the art that also falls outside the ordinary production and consumption of the city.

Punk rock had burst into my life with the force of revelation, though I cannot now call the revelation much more than a tempo and an insurrectionary intensity that matched the explosive pressure in my psyche. I was fifteen, and when I picture myself then, I see flames shooting up, see myself falling off the edge of the world, and am amazed I survived not the outside world but the inside one. Before and afterward, landscapes rural and wild would be the places that resonated most powerfully for me, but for the decade that started with my discovery of punk it was cities. The social I've often called a layer of baloney sandwiched between the bread of the physical and the spiritual, but that is only the most reductive form of the social, one that defines human possibility within narrow and predictable terms. Punk with its slam dancing and getting wasted and stage diving and standing in front of speakers that made your bones vibrate, with its political indignation and impulse to incite and express extreme states, was in collective revolt against this social. Like ruins, the social can become a wilderness in which the soul too becomes wild, seeking beyond itself, beyond its

||||||

imagination. And there is a specific kind of wildness, having to do with the erotic, the intoxicating, the transgressive, that is more easily located in cities than in wilderness. It has a time too, the time of youth, and of night.

I wonder now about Demeter and Persephone. Maybe Persephone was glad to run off with the king of death to his underground realm, maybe it was the only way she could break away from her mother, maybe Demeter was a bad parent the way that Lear was a bad parent, denying nature, including the nature of children to leave their parents. Maybe Persephone thought Hades was the infinitely cool older man who held the knowledge she sought, maybe she loved the darkness, the six months of winter, the sharp taste of pomegranates, the freedom from her mother, maybe she knew that to be truly alive death had to be part of the picture just as winter must. It was as the queen of hell that she became an adult and came into power. Hades's realm is called the underworld, and so are the urban realms of everything outside the law. And as in Hopi creation myths, where humans and other beings emerge from underground, so it's from the underground that culture emerges in this civilization.

In idyllic small towns I sometimes see teenagers looking out of place in their garb of desperation, the leftover tatters and stains and slashes of the fashion of my youth. For this phase of their life, the underworld is their true home, and in the grit and underbelly of a city they could find something that approximates it. Even the internal clock of adolescents changes, making them nocturnal creatures for at least a few years. All through childhood you grow toward life and then in adolescence, at the height of life, you begin to grow toward death. This fatality is felt as an enlargement to be welcomed and embraced, for the young in this culture enter adulthood as a prison, and death reassures them that there are exits. "I have been half in love with easeful death," said Keats who died at twenty-six and so were we, though the death we were in love with was only an idea then.

The title I gave our movie in the abandoned hospital was *A Cure for Living*. Not long before we began, I dreamed I was one of a long row of women on low beds in a stark, high-ceilinged vast room, more like a train station than a bedroom. The place was a military brothel. I think the premise must have been prompted in part by the band Joy Division, which pioneered a kind of melancholic dirge in the style of music that would be called industrial, but only issued a few albums before its lyricist and lead singer, Ian Curtis, hanged himself. A "joy division" was the Nazi term for a military brothel staffed by slaves. In my dream, the sexual labor was never explicit. All that happened is that, while I was in that long row, a man came up to me and handed me some small token. With that freely given gift I understood I was free to escape, as though some simple equation had been formed, that by dint of possession of that object I became distinct from the others, that because a choice had been made other choices could be made. In that dream, I started off, and the movie was to spin out that escape.

We never filmed that scene in the brothel, though we did make the gift, a ribbon he inscribed and I embroidered with an absurdist proverb from a novel my aunt had given me a few birthdays before, Vladimir Nabokov's *Pale Fire*. It declared, "The lost glove is happy." Perhaps the whole film was a gift that the filmmaker gave me, an encouragement to write my own escape, and the film too a ribbon as long as the thread with which Theseus traced his way out of the labyrinth in Crete. The hospital covered an entire city block with five stories of corridors and chambers. It was surrounded by one of those iron fences like a row of joined spears we'd scale before entering one of the cellar windows broken by squatters and explorers whose traces we occasionally found. Its intricate vastness reminded me of all those Borges tales about labyrinths and endless libraries, and part of the premise of my story line was that the hospital was thought to be infinite, an interior without an outside. It was a metaphor for an existential malady and an excuse for our heroine—me in an old white nightshirt—to keep wandering those decrepit corridors with their dusty light for our film. And it was an era of cinematic chases in the ruins and squalor of cities—*Road Warrior, Terminator, Blade Runner* all came out around this time.

One of the chief events of my escape that we filmed was an abduction by a mad doctor. The doctor believed that the soul had a physical location in the human body and kept performing fatal exploratory surgeries in search of it. I wrote him a long ranting monologue that could be taped and matched casually to the silent movie, thanks to the fact that the doctor wore a surgeon's mask. The character was partly borrowed from Djuna Barnes's novel *Nightwood,* another gift from the same aunt, and though *Nightwood* has never been part of the corpus of adolescence, in its description of erotic anguish and extreme states it could be. It's the garrulous cross-dressing garret dweller Doctor Matthew O'Connor I had in mind, who in answer to a heartbroken protagonist holds forth on love and on night for the length of a whole chapter in sentences even more pearl-encrusted than those of the rest of the book.

The moviemaker and I would find how and where to put our abilities to use in the coming years, but the film was only an excuse to linger with a sense of purpose in those exquisitely decrepit spaces. There was a morgue with rusted drawers the size of bodies and an operating theater with a tiled catwalk for overhead observation and ramps for gurneys and piles of old medical records telling of the ailments and cures of people long gone and strange rusty devices, but above all there was light filtered through dusty glass slanting into abandoned rooms and hallways. We used various friends in the movie, most of whom were as amateurish as we were. Only one of us was already an artist, Marine. She appeared in a vignette playing her cello while crouched on an iron bedframe strewn with sheet music, and from among that music she pulled the map that would take me out of the infinite hospital I had invented, a map the filmmaker had drawn.

The last time I saw Marine, the summer night we went out nightclubbing and made so many plans, we talked about the first time we saw each other. It had been just over seven years before, when she was nearly seventeen and I was not quite twenty-one, a few months before that movie. I saw her first, walking toward the suburban garage where her band was going to practice that spring afternoon, in her gray leather jacket with bass hefted in one hand, looking from a distance older and surer than she ever was. She and her succession of basses always seemed out of proportion to each other, and that she controlled something so imposing seemed as great a feat as, say, the girl acrobats atop their broad-backed horses in the circus. She had fingers like birthday candles, and she was proud of their calluses and of playing until they bled. She had moved to electric bass from cello, so outsize instruments were nothing new to her. She used to dream, she told me one of the first times we got together after that day in the garage, that her cello was a boat on which she was rowing away from her family. I didn't realize then how much the cello continued to figure in her life, how her violinist mother would cajole her into playing at the church services she herself played at every Sunday, though I did once go see Marine, her mother, and her haughty cocaine dealer friend play during midnight Mass at the Catholic church I used to linger at as a child, yearning for ritual and belonging.

Three things define her for me, her beauty, her talent, and her mercurial disposition—a natural evasiveness that tormented those who wanted to possess her and for me meant continual surprises and an inability to keep track of her. Marine was a delicate tomboy, sultry and pale, with the soft perfect skin of a child and fierce dark eyes better described as long than large. I remember a furtive look she had, of a cornered animal, and how elegant she'd become that last night. People wanted to capture her, like a wild thing, and take care of her, like a child. Beauty is often spoken of as though it only stirs lust or admiration, but the most beautiful people are so in a way that makes them look like destiny or fate or meaning, the heroes of a remarkable story. Desire for them is in part a desire for a noble destiny, and beauty can seem like a door to meaning as well as to pleasure. And yet such people are often nothing extraordinary except in their effect on others. Exceptional beauty and charm are among those gifts given by the sinister fairy at the christening. They give the bearer considerable sway over others, which can keep them so busy being a sort of siren on the rocks where others shipwreck that they forget that they themselves need to figure out where they are going. Marine had this quality of living in a story one might want to live in too, but she had ability, application, and boldness as well as beauty.

During the first few years after we met, we were close friends moving in similar circles, and she lived with me for a few months after moving out from a speed dealer's around the corner. Then she began to rove farther afield and I was swallowed up by other realms. Since I stayed in the same place throughout it all, she was always the one to call up with a new phone number or the news that she'd moved in with her mother and grandmother after another ménage or job fell through. The last time around, however, I knocked on her family's apartment door on a whim, found her just back from signing a record contract in L.A., and we picked up where we'd left off. That was early May. For the next few weeks we spoke regularly. In June Marine decided that she wanted to spend a Saturday night going around with me, and so we had an outing in which we mutually admired, rehashed the past, and made many plans for the future.

Marine had for me the glamour of a turbulent world I was never quite part of, of a talent utterly alien to me. Writing is the most disembodied art, and reading and writing are largely private and solitary experiences, so music and dance have always enchanted me as arts in which the body of the performer communicates directly to the audience, welding a kind of communion writers rarely experience. Some music has words, and rock had words that at times aspired to poetry, but the words were always sounds first, spoken to the body before the mind. Marine was too interested in being a musician to be a real three-chord punk rocker, so she gravitated toward the more ornate and less ideological realms of rock and roll proper. She had a surprising knowledge of obscure cultural things, not only the classical music that had been part of her family's life since a great-grandfather hung out with great composers. She'd suddenly describe someone as having a beard like De Sade's, employ an obscure term, wax sarcastic about the baroque era or Saint Anthony's temptations. I remember the delight she took in the profusely illustrated Audubon insect guide she acquired when she was living in Santa Monica, her fascination with the exotic species crawling around that subtropical global crossroads.

Perhaps rather than describe her as three characteristics, I could describe her as three places: the suburbs that made us and that we scorned and fled, the urban night she made into a home of sorts, and the pastoral world of a lyrical European culture and maybe of the hills past our childhood backyards. She never met her father, a musician her mother had an affair with while studying at a European conservatory, and she was named after the mistress of a composer. Her mother had been very young when Marine was born, and afterward they spent most of Marine's life with her grandparents. So she grew up with a mother who hadn't quite left home and with grandparents whose own musicianship had faded into sequestration and fret, with three people who didn't seem to work and didn't quite know what to do with a child. Her grandmother's screaming usually filled the house when I was

98

||||||

A
Field
Guide
to
Getting
Lost

in it—"the fishwife," Marine called her, and "the household furies doing their Verdi chorus." The scream was relentless, a litany of dangers and treacheries and savage reminders about hours and warm clothes, an interminable yowl about the barbarism of youth and viciousness of this one, a chant without a pause, a single wrathful sentence that must have gone on for at least a decade. It would raise up when Marine showed signs of leaving, break into telephone conversations, follow us down the stairs and out the door. Probably it had its origins in protective urges, but it had gone sour long ago.

Every time I heard from her, the situation was different—she'd be living with a different person, in or out of another band, employed, unemployed, on the verge of glory, on the mend from disaster, and somewhere around the end of her teens she mostly switched from male to female lovers, though there too nothing seemed certain. I don't know if stability and security bored her, if her plunges into chaos were part of the recklessness of the desultorily self-destructive, or if the dangers were simply accoutrements of the alluring—of drugs, adventures, music making, the incessant socializing of the drug-saturated music underworld. She had the nonchalance and style that mean so much to adolescents, who are urgently constructing a persona to meet the world, and this achievement is the antithesis of the openness that might make clear to self and others what one wants and needs. The currents of emotion that buffeted us were still invisible and unnamed.

When she was a teenager she did spectacular things with eye shadows, with azures and pinks and golds and other startling colors that made her eyes Byzantine mosaics; later she wore less and less eye makeup, and that last night she wasn't wearing any at all—it made her look old, she said. She was twenty-four. She had dyed her brown hair black, and with her pale, pale olive skin and fine bones she seemed almost to be dissolving into a photograph of herself, a perfect fleeting image. A gesture from that night: lifting her chin and, with closed eyes, pushing the strands of her hair from her forehead back with weary self-consciousness. We were both wearing black jeans and black T-shirts and boots and leather jackets. When we stopped at my house to listen to her demo tape and heft the manuscript of my first book, we preened in front of my mirror, and we danced together there and in the clubs. The man she was with, an older musician in her current band, watched indulgently. The night ended in a biker bar, where she lured the bar's big cat over to her lap while we drank our last round.

She looked radiant, and I believed her when she told me she was off drugs. We were out on a Saturday, and she was meeting a woman on Thursday; she wanted me and her male companion to come too. She was more insistent about this date than usual, and she called me up that Tuesday, partly to see if she'd left her shirt and sweater in my car and partly to confirm that she'd call me Thursday morning at ten to set up our ren-

dezvous. Such clarity and commitment were unusual, and so when she didn't call, I called her band's house, the house she'd been living at the last few weeks. Marine had died Tuesday night, the older musician said, and he was broken up over it. "Little Marine," he said, "I can't believe it."

A hundred adventures with Marine: the afternoon of my twenty-first birthday wandering with her and the filmmaker around the ruins of the vast Sutro Baths at the northwestern tip of San Francisco, where the waves smash hard enough to send the spray dozens of feet up; while walking on a local hillside in the greenness of early spring, stopping to throw rocks in the swimming pool of a world-famous old rock star who was giving young girls hard drugs for the usual reasons; wading in an icy forest stream until our feet were blue during a heat wave, after an expedition to fly her kite failed to turn up any winds; Marine about nineteen, blasé and impatient in a hospital gown after a speed binge resulted in dehydration and collapse; at home, cocking her head to one side to regard her baby pictures, declaring she looked exactly like Mussolini in them; us tossing the filmmaker's father's thorny backyard roses at her onstage, roses that the band's singer took as a tribute to herself; Marine and I climbing the wall of the Catholic cemetery down the street from her family's apartment as all the dogs at the adjacent school for the blind barked; coming home six months before her

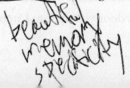

beautiful memory specificity

death to a message on my answering machine that said in tones of lighthearted wonder, "I love you. It's Marine!"

When I called back her band's house the next day to ask about funeral arrangements, I said, "But she seemed so happy, she seemed to have got everything together at last," and the musician said, "Marine was never happy for herself. She was happy for you." He told me that after our outing she'd gone home to take care of her grandmother while her mother went away and from there went to a party that Tuesday night. At the party she took something that killed her. It wasn't surprising and it wasn't quite real. I kept thinking it was a bizarre mistake or a made-up story, until I called her mother, who told me how beautifully made up Marine's corpse was and urged me to go see her at the funeral chapel. This, with her cigarettes still in my ashtray, her hair still in my brush, her clothes still in my car, her voice still in my ears, so soon after we'd been looking at ourselves together in my mirror and she the more lithe, the more fluidly beautiful of the two. That Saturday I suddenly walked out of a symposium and went to the chapel.

I'd never been to such a place before. A Georgian portico, a long hallway with doors on both sides, a family with children gathering for a funeral there looking at me doubtfully. The hallway confused me until I noticed lecterns with guest books outside each doorway. The book at the last lectern had Marine's name written on it, and the curtained glass door was ajar, so I stepped

it's within you, that kingdom of god

through. The room was a dim mock-chapel. There was a strange hush, there were huge candles and a stained-glass window through which dull, faint light filtered above a vast, ornate, ivory casket like a pastry, set on a bier like an altar, inside which there was a little boy vampire. From the doorway, in profile, she looked tranquil, a sleeper. Up close in that light, she looked only half-familiar, and I realized how much her constant flickering motion had been a part of the impression she made. The coffin was lined with white satin, soft as a bed, and I found myself whispering, "Marine, Marine, Marine, wake up."

Her mother called me up every once in a while for a few years afterward, and during one call told me that the night Marine died was her wedding night. The man she married was young and well-off, halfway between their ages, and Marine had talked about how much she hated him, though she never mentioned the marriage. Her mother came home the morning after the wedding to the celebratory bottle of champagne that Marine had bought her and to her own mother saying, "You must be strong, you're going to have to be very strong." With this revelation, the facts reordered themselves again: it seemed that, in the bitter upset of a marriage that might put home out of bounds, Marine was reckless not to escape but because her return was blocked. I folded up the violet shirt and sweater she'd left in my car and put them in the chest at the foot of my bed. They are still there. In the shirt pocket I found the crumpled wrapper of a Tootsie Pop.

This era came rushing back to me a few years ago when I walked into a New York gallery full of the photographs of Peter Hujar, who died of AIDS in 1986. I had been looking at thoroughly contemporary art in the several galleries that preceded this momentous entrance, art that was sleek, shiny, clever, art about design issues, fashion, disaffection, art that was in some ways about the smooth surface of the new city that had replaced the cityscape that so moved me in Hujar's work. The very texture was different. In Hujar's saturated black-and-white prints of animals, outcasts, eccentrics, and ruinous places, the world was rough in every sense. Its surfaces were porous, decrepit, sensuous, full of age and what seemed an ability to absorb: to absorb light, meaning, emotion. The city had mystery and danger of the sort urban renewal pledges to remove. Not far from the gallery was Chelsea Piers, now "a family place," a high-end sports and exercise complex, pricy, regulated, safe, and predictable, full of healthy people simulating activities like golf and climbing that really only happen elsewhere. It is in a profound way synthetic, a synthesis of purposes and a simulation of places, though it may yet yield to ruin again.

The Chelsea Piers Web site steers clear of all the history between 1976 and 1992, when its current phase began. "But the Chelsea Piers just sat there rusting in the harbor air until destiny called them back," is all it said, but they didn't just sit there. During those years every kind of sexual outlaw and pariah made themselves at home in this temporary autonomous zone, sadomasochists in leather and transvestites in fishnet and homeless people and junkies. Chelsea Piers was the place Peter Hujar photographed and his protégé David Wojnarowicz (who died of AIDs in 1992) cruised and wrote about: "Paper from old shipping lines scattered all around like bomb blasts among wrecked pieces of furniture; three-legged desks, a naugahyde couch of mint-green turned upside down, and small rectangles of light and wind and river over the far wall. I lean towards him, pushing him against the wall, lifting my pale hands up beneath his sweater. . . . In the warehouse just before dark, passed along the hallways and photographed the various graffiti on the walls, some of hermaphrodites and others of sharp-faced thugs smoking cigarettes . . ." Something about the emotional, erotic, aesthetic, and ethical intensity of Wojnarowicz seems inseparable from this kind of place, for if he— queer, punk, desperado, activist—was the quintessential artist of his time it was because the time was about this kind of place, one that was ruinous, bleak, but somehow still imbued with a romantic outlaw sense of possibility, of freedom, even the freedom to be idealistic, idealistic in the bitter vein of the Sex Pistols' "No Future," perhaps, but idealistic all the same.

"A nuclear error but I have no fear," sang the Clash, "'cause London is drowning and I—I live by the river." It was the era of Reagan's nuclear brinksmanship, and the postnuclear ruins were in every imagination. "The living will envy the dead," was the phrase Nuclear

Freeze activists recited like a mantra, and books, articles, a made-for-TV movie anticipated what kind of ruin the Northern Hemisphere could become. I had always anticipated living in this postnuclear world, and when I thought of my future I wondered whether survival skills or a graduate degree was more germane. Though the ruins were imagined as prophetic architecture of the future, they were the essence of their time. The great industrial cities were becoming something else: San Francisco and New York were almost done losing their ports to more suburban sites, and the small industries of the inner cities were being replaced by artists and the smooth affluence that sometimes follows and imitates artists.

We are now at the beginning of an era whose constructions are far scarier than ruins. In the time of which I write, the new silicon-based life forms were sneaking into every interstice without setting off alarms that all would be utterly changed in a way far more insidious than nuclear war, that they would bring a new wealth that would erase the ruins. In the 1980s we imagined apocalypse because it was easier than the strange complicated futures that money, power, and technology would impose, intricate futures hard to exit. In the same way, teenagers imagine dying young because death is more imaginable than the person that all the decisions and burdens of adulthood may make of you. Then I thought of Marine's death as the end of my youth because it signaled the end of my connection to that underworld, but it might instead have been because death became real.

Everything had changed for me in the couple of years that ended with Marine's death: my father died in a distant country; things that had been too perilous to see before surfaced, and so I wrestled with some highly educational demons; I quit my job and embarked on the life I'm still living, that of an independent writer; and the filmmaker moved to Los Angeles to begin a successful career in the entertainment industry, a transition that made it clear that we were heading in different directions, and so we parted. I lost a whole life and gradually gained another one, more open and more free. Though I think of the 1980s as my most urban phase, Marine and I, who had both grown up in that suburban county of beautiful hills, kept one foot in the rural or the wild, for that direction was also an escape.

I think now that the suburbs were a kind of tranquilizer for the generation before us, if topography can be a drug. The blandness of ranch houses, the soothing lines of streets curving into cul-de-sacs, the homogeneity, the repetition, the pretty, vacant names were designed to erase the desperation of poverty and strife, to erase tenements and barracks and migrant camps and sharecropper shacks. What they wanted to erase, we unearthed and made into our underground culture, our refuge, our identity. We were shaking that trance off us and going out in pursuit of the world of our grandparents, us kids not so remote from a lost Europe, from the Second World War, from desperation and privation. That was what the city offered, a sharp antidote, the possibility of being fully awake, surrounded by all possibilities, some of which we'd learn the hard way were terrible. I am still a city dweller, but in those days when everything changed I first began going deep in the other direction. Another world was opening up to me in which night was for sleep and, far from city lights, for stars. I got to know the Milky Way and the sharpness of the shadows the full moon casts in the desert.

I wonder now about Marine's abandon. In a way it seems brave to me, this charging into adventure without fear of consequences. Or was it a desperation in which there were more terrible things than death, a desire so urgent for the anesthesia, distraction, and sense of destiny drugs seem to offer, even a desire for death? Was I cowardly not to want to explore the farther reaches of consciousness, afraid of getting lost, of being unable to return? I had been on my own since I turned seventeen, and that early independence made me old: I was never sure anyone would pick up the pieces if I fell apart, and I thought of consequences. The young live absolutely in the present, but a present of drama and recklessness, of acting on urges and running with the pack. They bring the fearlessness of children to acts with adult consequences, and when something goes wrong they experience the shame or the pain as an eternal present too. Adulthood is made up of a prudent anticipation and a philosophical memory that make you

||||||

navigate more slowly and steadily. But fear of making mistakes can itself become a huge mistake, one that prevents you from living, for life is risky and anything less is already loss. I missed a lot of adventures that way early on, but I know that there were many paths I could have taken, and madness and misery lay down some of them, just as death was down one of Marine's, closing off the others her talents and passions might have taken her down.

On a few occasions a few years later, I would enjoy the metallic taste of poppies in various states of refinement and their effect of turning me into something almost reptilian. Opiates seem to kill not merely physical but existential pain, turning you into a cool spectator of your own sensations and desires and of passing time, as languorous as all those images of divans and draperies and long pipes had promised. Though in yet another version of Marine's death, I heard that it was not the heroin that killed her but a shot of speed her companions gave her to "wake her up": the two together are a deadly combination, and in this version she died of cowards unwilling to risk any legal consequences from calling the paramedics who could've revived her with a single injection. I cannot say now whether it was a murder, a suicide, an accident, or all those things at once. Marine plunged into the unknown again and again, but she kept returning home, while I trudged on in a straight line away from where I'd started.

The

Blue

of

Distance

Blue was the title I gave a compilation tape I made a dozen years ago, and some of the songs were about sadness, some about the sky, some about both. Every once in a while I made a collection like that, mostly to be listened to on long road trips, and in them I tried to define what it was that moved me in the music I chose. An earlier one had been called *Geography Lessons, Mostly Tragic,* and there too I had tried to get at something about the evocation of place and its emotional resonance in that music. A compilation about rivers and drinking, about drowning from the inside and out, I called *The Entirely Liquid Mr. North,* after the fatally alcoholic composer Abe North in F. Scott Fitzgerald's *Tender Is the Night,* though the songs were southern. In *Blue,* most of the music had some relationship to the blues, as if the music was going back to its origins in longing and the blue of distance.

I had discovered country and western music a few years before—not the modern stuff that is mostly sentimental pop with fiddles and a twang, but the older tunes that plumbed the dark depths of emotional experience. I had grown up in immigrant, coastal, liberal culture far removed from the realm of this music and been taught to despise the stuff as banal, as trashy, as vulgar without ever really heeding it. When the music burst upon me all of a sudden one spring, I was stunned to find out that the most popular songs often were, like the stories of Edgar Allan Poe and Katherine Anne Porter, a kind of southern gothic in love with tragedy and topography. Thinking about it now, I wonder about an era when a wrenching poetics of loss possessed the airwaves and wonder too about how it slid over into the true banality of upbeat contemporary country (though there are still great balladeers around the edges of that genre).

The songs that worked their way into my blood were like short stories compressed into a few stanzas and a refrain; they always spanned and layered time. The music was haunted, was about distant memory, was about the dead and gone or at the very least aimed at a beloved far beyond earshot. Like writing, the music was solitary, talking to itself in that solitude of composition and contemplation, in the free flow of time that is before, after, between, but somehow never quite the now of a thriving romance, and perhaps this was also the time of my long summer drives, of driving six hundred, a thousand miles in a day, of unrolling again and again like movies, like stories, like the stories small children demand for reassurance, the sequences of Highway 40 through Arizona and New Mexico, 80 and 50 through Nevada and Utah, of 58 and 285 through the California desert, of many secondary highways and other roads, roads whose mesas and diners were always the same and whose light and clouds and weather never were.

And this wasn't the obscure or alternative stuff, nec-
essarily. At a flea market, I picked up a cassette of Tanya
Tucker's early hits for a quarter or fifty cents, back
when I was first poking around at what to me was a
whole new continent. The cassette was like an anthology of stories. A former beauty walked around town,
mad from loss, and stuck in a moment that had evaporated away long ago, carrying a suitcase and waiting for
a man who had abandoned her long before. A nameless
voice asked her nameless lover, "Would you lay with
me (in a field of stone)," summoning up a bizarre picture of lovers in one of those unplowable granitic pas-
tures, and the intensity of need seemed to be all the
explanation the strange request required. ("Walking
After Midnight," Patsy Cline's huge 1957 hit, is unset-
tlingly peculiar in the same way: she walks—in the
words of Don Hecht and Alan Block—along the highway in the middle of the night to say that she loves the
"you" of the song, not a very domesticated or reasonable
or even straightforward way of saying anything, and
the obliqueness of the means is in direct proportion to
the impossibility of really saying it to the unnamed, irrecoverable beloved in this landscape of loneliness.) A
woman recalled the man who had approached her when
she was a child. He asked her her mother's name and
whether she ever spoke of a place called New Orleans
and, for bothering a child, was thrown into jail. Near the
present in which the song is sung, the questioner died,
and on his corpse was the note from her mother an-
nouncing her birth, so that the one meeting between fa-

ther and daughter had been a catastrophe of nonrecognition, of the failure to connect that is so much the material of these songs that layer time like dirt on a grave.

They were always about someone recalling a tragedy that unfolded long ago, generally about someone else, so that a sort of haze of remoteness lay over the once wrenching events, the kind of time that Joseph Conrad invoked when he'd set up a narrator on a docked ship telling a tale of another man in another ocean long before, an unresolved riddle to be revisited. The quintessential song in this vein and the one I love best is "Long Black Veil," which the protagonist sings from beyond the grave, ten years after he was hanged for a crime he did not commit as his best friend's wife silently watched him die. They had been together, in bed, but neither would invoke the alibi that would have saved him. And so, as the famous refrain goes, she walks these hills in a long black veil "and visits my grave when the night winds wail." Even Bobbie Gentry's 1967 "Ode to Billy Joe," that megahit in which the girl protagonist may have pushed her lover off the Tallahatchie Bridge (below Choctaw Ridge), has something of that sense of looking at ghosts and wraiths in the rearview mirror of irrecoverable time, irrecoverable loss and error.

The protagonists were often anonymous, nameless, described in only the vaguest terms. A man, a woman, a beloved dead a long time ago, a faithless wife, a cruel husband, a hope abandoned, a dream glimpsed once and lost. But the territory in which these dramas played

themselves out were evoked in detail over and over again, and if they were tragic songs about the failure of human love, they were also love songs about places, whose names were recited like incantations and ca-
resses. The names or just the facts of bridges, mountains, valleys, towns, states, rivers (lots of rivers), highways were recalled in reverie, and psychic states themselves became places, "Lost Highway" and "Lonely Street." So though they were overtly love songs, in most of them the landscape was a deeper anchor for being and the object of another, more enduring love. The grave, the town hall light, the hills, and the gallows are all more vivid than the protagonists of "Long Black Veil." Perhaps it's that you can't go back in time, but you can return to the scenes of a love, of a crime, of happiness, and of a fatal decision; the places are what remain, are what you can possess, are what is immortal. They become the tangible landscape of memory, the places that made you, and in some way you too become them. They are what you can possess and what in the end possesses you.

In my old Tanya Tucker cassette, Brownsville, San Antonio, Memphis, New Orleans, and Pecos were the only proper names mentioned, though streets, fields, rivers, stores, jails, ferries, and other locations also showed up. The people were nameless and sometimes the women began to dissolve into places, like those tragic figures the gods would turn into rosebushes or fountains to stabilize their grief. There was, of course, the jilted bride called Delta Dawn, and far more scorchingly, there was the young rape victim who withdrew into herself and became known as No Man's Land. She grew up to be a beauty, a nurse, and one day found herself called upon to nurse her rapist—the song is vague about the details, but she seems to have watched him die rather than treating him, "and now his soul is walking / In No Man's Land." It's a terrifying song, about the damage people can do to each other and about the way the rapist comes to possess her twice, once as the soul who haunts the limbo she has become.

The places in which any significant event occurred become embedded with some of that emotion, and so to recover the memory of the place is to recover the emotion, and sometimes to revisit the place uncovers the emotion. Every love has its landscape. Thus place, which is always spoken of as though it only counts when you're present, possesses you in its absence, takes on another life as a sense of place, a summoning in the imagination with all the atmospheric effect and association of a powerful emotion. The places inside matter as much as the ones outside. It is as though in the way places stay with you and that you long for them they become deities—a lot of religions have local deities, presiding spirits, geniuses of the place. You could imagine that in those songs Kentucky or the Red River is a spirit to which the singer prays, that they mourn the dreamtime before banishment, when the singer lived among the gods who were not phantasms but geography, matter, earth itself.

There is a voluptuous pleasure in all that sadness, and

I wonder where it comes from, because as we usually construe the world, sadness and pleasure should be far apart. Is it that the joy that comes from other people always risks sadness, because even when love doesn't fail, mortality enters in; is it that there is a place where sadness and joy are not distinct, where all emotion lies together, a sort of ocean into which the tributary streams of distinct emotions go, a faraway deep inside; is it that such sadness is only the side effect of art that describes the depths of our lives, and to see that described in all its potential for loneliness and pain is beautiful? There are songs of insurgent power; they are essentially what rock and roll, an outgrowth of one strain of the blues, does best, these songs of being young and at the beginning of the world, full of a sense of your own potential. Country, at least the old stuff, has mostly been devoted instead to aftermath, to the hard work it takes to keep going or the awareness that comes after it is no longer possible to go on. If it is deeper than rock it is because failure is deeper than success. Failure is what we learn from, mostly.

All those summer drives, no matter where I was going, to a person, a project, an adventure, or home, alone in the car with my social life all before and behind me, I was suspended in the beautiful solitude of the open road, in a kind of introspection that only outdoor space generates, for inside and outside are more intertwined than the usual distinctions allow. The emotion stirred by the landscape is piercing, a joy close to pain when the blue is deepest on the horizon or the clouds are doing those spectacular fleeting things so much easier to recall than to describe. Sometimes I thought of my apartment in San Francisco as only a winter camp and home as the whole circuit around the West I travel a few times a year and myself as something of a nomad (nomads, contrary to current popular imagination, have fixed circuits and stable relationships to places; they are far from being the drifters and dharma bums that the word *nomad* often connotes nowadays). This meant that it was all home, and certainly the intense emotion that, for example, the sequence of mesas alongside the highway for perhaps fifty miles west of Gallup, N.M., and a hundred miles east has the power even as I write to move me deeply, as do dozens of other places, and I have come to long not to see new places but to return and know the old ones more deeply, to see them again. But if this was home, then I was both possessor of an enchanted vastness and profoundly alienated.

So were the people in those songs, and it seemed that place-names had an evocative power there that they did in my life: I love to hear people say those names. Once when I was living in New Mexico, a student who'd lived in my part of California would charm and mesmerize me by saying, "Sebastopol, Occidental, Freestone, Gravenstein Highway, Petaluma . . ." Now, it's the New Mexico names that have the most power over me, Golondrinas, Mora, Chacon, Trampas, Chimayo, Nambe, Rio en Medio, Canyoncito, Stanley, Moriarty, the East Mountains, Cerrillos, Cerro Pelon. There's a whole genre of song that began in the blues that consists largely of place-names, a recitative of geography, of

||||||

which the famous "Route 66" is only the most popular. (Perhaps they came from conductors' cries on the railroads, as does the list in the bluegrass tune "Orange Blossom Special"; perhaps travel and lists are inevitably wed, so that a music of restlessness paces itself in place-names.) An outsider's insightful approximation of its essence is "Wanted Man," which Bob Dylan wrote in 1969 and Johnny Cash most famously covered. It's a boastful list of all the places a criminal is wanted, a recitation that includes Albuquerque and Tallahassee and Baton Rouge and Buffalo, a confusion of being desired with being hunted that has unsettling intimations about the motives for committing a crime.

That life is a journey is a given in these songs whose background after all is the urbanization of rural whites and northern migration of southern blacks, but the intense love of place frames this journey not as an enlightenment narrative of discovery of the unknown but an insular tale of loss of the formative terra cognita that exists in the song only as memory, a map written in the darkness of your guts, readable in a cross section of your autopsied heart. Nobody gets over anything; time doesn't heal any wounds; if he stopped loving her today, as one of George Jones's most famous songs has it, it's because he's dead. The landscape in which identity is supposed to be grounded is not solid stuff; it's made out of memory and desire, rather than rock and soil, as are the songs.

People look into the future and expect that the forces of the present will unfold in a coherent and predictable way, but any examination of the past reveals that the circuitous routes of change are unimaginably strange. No logic and no prophesy could explain the evolution of the whale from an ancient aquatic creature through eons on land and then back in the sea to become something utterly different from anything that could survive on the surface of the earth. The music called the blues is as good an example as any of the unlikely, an evolution of African music in the southeastern American landscape, inflected by slavery and exposure to the English language, European instruments, and, perhaps, Irish, Scottish, and English ballads—the passionate melancholy of murder ballads and songs about abandoned maidens and bloody revenges. The term *blue* comes from an old English word for melancholy or for sadness, blue moods, blue devils, the blues, first tracked to 1555 in my etymological dictionary.

The world from which the blues came is largely vanished. Not half a century after slavery it came out of severely limited choices and limited movement, and to read the early biographies is to collect pictures of sharecroppers in small shacks surrounded by cotton; of prisoners, children, everyone at hard labor; of dust; of the floods of the Mississippi and the vagaries of the law; of a society in which people who had once been slaves were still far from free. Some of the people who came from that world settled in the neighborhood I've lived in most of my adult life and told me about it, but they are dying out, one by one, and their great-grandchildren are listening to something else entirely, though the local churches still sing gospel. The blues are a kind of captivity narrative, but the white captivity narratives often told of people whose capture was either temporary or became full acceptance into a new society. The blues defined a kind of perpetual internal exile of people who couldn't go back, though leaving the South is a subject of a lot of blues songs, without white country music's hankering for the places left behind. In these terms, even nostalgia and homesickness are privileges not granted to everyone.

Poverty and racism aren't vanished but the self-containment of the rural black community was broken up by emigration, by a degree of desegregation, and most of all by the transformation of the world by cheap transportation and pervasive mass media, by the deterioration of the local almost everywhere. It's as though a sort of specific gravity dissipated, but before it did, it pressed together these disparate forces into an intensity of expression the way that tremendous weight and pressure turn soil and mineral into gemstone. The blues proper, the blues as the species existed in 1933, is frail and precious, a style that often seems anachronistic or nostalgic itself (with a largely white audience nowadays), but it spread to become the ancestor of most modern popular music, one way or another.

In some ways the blues took over the world, and the melancholy specific to the post-slavery South became something universal, or a universal melancholy found a specific channel for its expression. The country songs about place I collected were in some ways the blues—I think of how many songs Hank Williams wrote that were explicitly framed as the blues—but it was as though you could take that color literally, imagine the original blues as a deep color, passionate and defiant, indigo, azure, sapphire, diluted into the brooding melancholy of these white songs of loss and backward glances, into the blue of distance.

There is a story within a story by Isak Dinesen about the color blue that seemed like another one of these songs, this one without the voice and music that make them so visceral, but with their sense of looking across great distances of time, space, and self. I remembered it and looked all through her books again and again for it in vain, this lost story about the color blue, and then one day did a Web search for Isak Dinesen and blue and found that it was the story the writer tells the sailors inside "The Young Man with the Carnation," a tale about a writer's crisis of despair for the duration of one night, a crisis that ends in the morning with him making a pact with God. God makes a covenant that "I will not measure you out any more distress than you need to write your books. Do you want any less than that?" The story only lasts a page and a half, so that it has the sketchiness of the songs—"Long Black Veil" in the version I looked up has the same number of lines as a sonnet but the skeleton of a novel within those lines.

Dinesen was herself an emigrant to Africa, and something of the hybridity of the blues might be in the influence African storytelling had on her talent for tales that are more luminous and unexpected than ordinary short stories, more elaborate and credible than fables and fairy tales. In the story within a story I rediscovered, an old English aristocrat who had served his country no longer cared for anything but collecting blue china, and so he traveled the world with his young daughter to do so. It's a telling detail, for that china was already part of the export market, so that the Dutch and Chinese both made ware that approximated what Europeans thought Chinese ceramics should look like, that blue-and-white stuff whose most familiar imagery is also a small tale of tragedy, the blue willow pattern of birds, trees, water, and separated lovers, like the items of a song you could drink from, teacups that would always be a cup of sorrow. Their ship was wrecked, the daughter was left behind in the evacuation, and at the last minute a sailor took her into an overlooked lifeboat and for nine days the two were alone together on the sea.

After they were rescued, Dinesen through her fictional young writer continues, her father banished the sailor beyond reach, to the other side of the world, and all the rescued castaway wanted to do was collect blue china. "In her search she told the people with whom she dealt that she was looking for a particular blue colour and would pay any price for it. But although she bought many hundred blue jars and bowls, she would always after a time put them aside and say: 'Alas, alas, it is not the right blue.' Her father, when they had sailed for many years, suggested to her that perhaps the colour which she sought did not exist. 'O God, Papa,' said she, 'how can you speak so wickedly? Surely there

123

The
Blue
of
Distance

must be some of it left from the time when all the world was blue.'" Years passed, decades, her father died, and finally, a merchant brought her an old blue jar looted from the Chinese emperor's summer palace. When she saw it she said that now she could die, and when she died, her heart would be cut out and put in the blue jar. "And everything will be as it was then. All shall be blue round me, and in the midst of the blue world my heart will be innocent and free, and will beat gently . . ."

Two

Arrowheads

Once I loved a man who was a lot like the desert, and before that I loved the desert. It wasn't particular things but the space between them, that abundance of absence, that is the desert's invitation. There the geology that underlies lusher landscapes is exposed to the eye, and this gives it a skeletal elegance, just as its harsh conditions—the vast distances between water, the many dangers, the extremes of heat and cold—keep you in mind of your mortality. But the desert is made first and foremost out of light, at least to the eye and the heart, and you quickly learn that the mountain range twenty miles away is pink at dawn, a scrubby green at midday, blue in evening and under clouds. The light belies the bony solidity of the land, playing over it like emotion on a face, and in this the desert is intensely alive, as the apparent mood of mountains changes hourly, as places that are flat and stark at noon fill with shadows and mystery in the evening, as darkness becomes a reservoir from which the eyes drink, as clouds promise rain that comes like passion and leaves like redemption, rain that delivers itself with thunder, with lightning, with a rise of scents in this place so pure that moisture, dust, and the various bushes all have their own smell in the sudden humidity. Alive with the primal forces of rock,

129

weather, wind, light, and time in which biology is only an uninvited guest fending for itself, gilded, dwarfed, and threatened by its hosts. It was the vastness that I loved and an austerity that was also voluptuous. And the man?

I went to visit him in his home deep in the Mojave one evening in late spring. We had met once, and several months later he called me up claiming that he was looking for the phone number of the friend who'd introduced us, kept me on the phone for an hour or more, and ended by telling me to come by when I was next in the vicinity, and so I did. We talked from the bright light of early evening into the darkness of the first warm night of the season, and the soft breeze itself was a delight to me, playing over arms and legs that no longer needed to be wrapped up against the night. We talked while the full moon mounted in the sky, words filling up the narrow space between us, as much a buffer as a link. Hours passed and then suddenly at my foot there was a wriggle of the soil. A kangaroo mouse emerged, a creature that I have never otherwise seen except fleeing at a distance. I put my hand on the man's shoulder to call his attention to this surprise, and we fell silent and watched the strangely fearless mouse do its work for a long time, then resumed the conversation more slowly and more softly as the creature continued to refine its tunnel entrance and the mound of gravelly earth at its mouth, indifferent to our presence. Bats swooped down and snatched invisible meals from the air, and coyotes began to howl, more of them, closer and more persistently than I've ever heard before or since, a whole orchestra of drawn-out cries into the dawn.

With other men you get to know their families, with this unhurried man who seemed like a desert hermit, animals seemed to fill that place, and they were always around his home. Solitude in the city is about the lack of other people or rather their distance beyond a door or wall, but in remote places it isn't an absence but the presence of something else, a kind of humming silence in which solitude seems as natural to your species as to any other, words strange rocks you may or may not turn over. I have lived in other deserts, but I have never lived in one so alive with animals. Cottontails and jackrabbits and darting, bobbing desert quail were always nearby, and early in the morning I would see the rabbits dance with each other and jump straight into the air in play. Often a late-afternoon coyote strolled through the yard, a bobcat gave me a cool look there once, the neighbors saw a mountain lion in it, and many mornings a pair of roadrunners chased each other in the driveway.

On our second date he told me that when he'd woken up there was a rattlesnake outside, too cold to move in the early morning chill, so he had picked it up on a shovel and moved it into the garage, hoping it would go after the pack rat eating the wiring there. I was surprised and smitten by this response so counter to what most people hope for from snakes: distance. He had a passion for snakes, and on each of our early rendezvous seemed to have another story to tell. One was about driving from the Mojave to the mountains on summer evenings, going slowly so that he could see the snakes who'd come out to bask on the asphalt that held warmth longer into the night than anything else, see them and pick them up and take them to safety. He had seen a gopher snake sit outside a rabbit hole and eat each of the young as it emerged, seen snakes making love, rising high into the air to twine around each other, and he seemed to run into rattlesnakes regularly. One day he came home and told me in the hushed tone I'd learned was tenderness of seeing a baby rattler no thicker than his finger. After that first rendezvous I continued my journey to my original destination, another desert where I would stay alone and write. A few days later, the longest day of the year, I was walking up a little dirt track when I remembered what I'd dreamed of the night before, a snake, and as I said the word to myself, I looked down and saw my right foot was poised to come down on a fat little rattler with a buttony tail, flicking its tongue and wriggling along.

What is the message that wild animals bring, the message that seems to say everything and nothing? What is this message that is wordless, that is nothing more or less than the animals themselves—that the world is wild, that life is unpredictable in its goodness and its danger, that the world is larger than your imagination? I remember a day when he was out working and I was alone in his house writing. I heard a raven fly by in air so still that each slow stroke of its wings was distinctly audible. I wondered then and wonder now how I could give all this up for what cities and people have to offer, for it ought to be less terrible to be lonely than to have stepped out of this sense of a symbolic order that the world of animals and celestial light offers, but writing is lonely enough, a confession to which there will be no immediate or commensurate answer, an opening statement in a conversation that falls silent or takes place long afterward without the author. But the best writing appears like those animals, sudden, self-possessed, telling everything and nothing, words approaching wordlessness. Maybe writing is its own desert, its own wilderness.

There are moments of harmony that rise to the level of serendipity, coincidence, and beyond, and certain passages of time that seem dense with such incidents. Summers and deserts seem best for them. I remember lying in the shade of my truck in the Great Basin reading *The Divine Comedy*. As I finished the last lines of the Paradiso, when Dante approaches the light and is turned like a wheel by "the love which moves the sun and other stars," a car pulled up. The Franciscan father who ministered to Skid Row characters in Las Vegas and to the cause of peace in the desert stepped out, a comic saint with a thick Breton accent who seemed to have driven up straight out of paradise into that desert that resonated so much with Dante's tale. Or a time walking in another desert when I thought of the obsidian bird-point arrowhead I'd found in that area the year before, then recollected the creamy chert arrowhead a man had given me since then, and with the latter picture in my head looked down to see its twin, another pale arrowhead with a wide base, a perfect match two thousand miles away six months later, so startling a coincidence that my sense of cause and effect was rattled for a day. Countless times when I traveled hundreds of miles to meet a friend who arrived simultaneously at our remote destination, when what we were looking for appeared unexpectedly, when two people spoke the same thought in the same words at once. Such moments seem to mean that you have surrendered to the story being told and are following the story line rather than trying to tell it yourself, your puny voice interrupting and arguing with fate, nature, the gods.

One perfect midsummer day three years after that evening I'd arrived in the hermit's life and he in mine, I had gotten up early in that shack whose back bedroom window opened onto one of the most spectacular views I've ever seen and whose kitchen window was up against a slope, so that as I filled the kettle I was eye to eye with a young cottontail, unafraid as I remained unseen through the glass, its eye a round black mirror for creosote bush and window frame. The yard was full of cottontails that day, and then I found a huge desert tortoise strolling up to chomp on the prickly pears, as though we had stumbled into the fable of the tortoise and the hare, whose dispositions I often imagined as the hermit's and mine, he so reserved, deliberate, patient, I so quick and high-strung. I told the neighbor

and the hermit, and they came out and, in the manner
of men, let on that they had seen tortoises as big. Hav[e]
you ever seen one bigger, I asked, and they fell silent,
watching the creature open a beaky mouth and cut cac-
tus with slow menace. That evening we went to feed
the cats of an acquaintance who was away, and inside
the house we found the three creatures stalking a mourn-
ing dove fluttering bloody around the big room. While
I fended off the cats, he caught the creature. It vanished
into his hands, and this seemed to calm it until we got
outside. He raised his hands up and the dove flew into
the last light, more alive than we'd hoped.

An idyll like that wasn't made to last. For a while it
was forever, and then things started to fall apart. There
isn't a story to tell, because a relationship is a story you
construct together and take up residence in, a story as
sheltering as a house. You invent this story of how your
destinies were made to entwine like porch vines, you
adjust to a big view in this direction and no view in
that, the doorway that you have to duck through and
the window that is jammed, how who you think you
are becomes a factor of who you think he is and who he
thinks you are, a castle in the clouds made out of the
moist air exhaled by dreamers. It's a shock to find yourself outdoors and alone again, hard to imagine that you
could ever live in another house, big where this one was
small, small where it was big, hard when your body has
learned all the twists and turns of the staircase so that
you could walk it in your sleep, hard when you have

built it from scratch and called it home, hard to imagine building again. But you lit the fire that burned it down yourself.

A happy love is a single story, a disintegrating one is two or more competing, conflicting versions, and a disintegrated one lies at your feet like a shattered mirror, each shard reflecting a different story, that it was wonderful, that it was terrible, if only this had, if only that hadn't. The stories don't fit back together, and it's the end of stories, those devices we carry like shells and shields and blinkers and occasionally maps and compasses. The people close to you become mirrors and journals in which you record your history, the instruments that help you know yourself and remember yourself, and you do the same for them. When they vanish so does the use, the appreciation, the understanding of those small anecdotes, catchphrases, jokes: they become a book slammed shut or burnt. Though I came out of this house transformed, stronger and surer than I had been, and carrying with me more knowledge of myself, of men, of love, of deserts and wildernesses.

The stories shatter. Or you wear them out or leave them behind. Over time the story or the memory loses its power. Over time you become someone else. Only when the honey turns to dust are you free. I went away for the summer, back to the desert I had been headed for when I detoured his way the evening of the kangaroo mouse, all those years before. Heartbreak is a little like falling in love, in the way it charges everything

with a kind of incandescence, as though the beloved has stepped away and your gaze now rests with all the same intensity on all the items of the view that close-up person blocked. Out in the small house in that desert one of the insects called walking sticks took up residence on one of the windows, and after I poked it to make sure it wasn't a stray bit of straw, I took to talking to it occasionally, so companionable was it. A spider with an image like a foolishly smiling face on her big white abdomen dwelt in the eaves over the door I passed through to write. Paper wasps built nests in those eaves. All around the little house Mexican grasshoppers flung out their wings, black, yellow, and scarlet, vivid like butterflies while they flew, drab again when they landed. Bumblebees landed on coneflowers that dipped halfway to the ground under their weight. Occasionally a velvet ant upholstered in red or yellow plush walked by, and black beetles with a forward tilt left tiny trails in the dust.

There were lizards in abundance, and when they climbed the screens of the windows, I was delighted as I'd always been by the azure stripes on the undersides of the species we always called bluebellies. They kept drowning in the horse trough under the drainpipe, where they would float pale and hapless like sailors in a Victorian shipwreck poem. In the distance was the celestial drama of summer thunderstorms, clouds assembling in vast arrays that demonstrated how far the sky went and how high, that shifted from the bundled white cumulus into the deep blue of storm clouds, and when we were lucky, poured down rain and lightning and shafts of light and vapor trails like a violent redemption. It was as though the whole world consisted of the tiny close-up realm of these creatures and the vast distances of heaven, as though my own scale had been eliminated along with the middle ground, and this too is one of the austere luxuries of the desert.

In the fall, I went back to the city and began to compose a story in my head. I was already working on a book then, or I would have written it down. Now it is as decayed as a real book might be after being buried or abandoned, and when I think of the scraps that remain, I wonder what weather in the mind so erodes such things.

Alfred Hitchcock's film *Vertigo* is sometimes described as a love letter to San Francisco, though its subject is a romance between the protagonist, an ex-detective with vertigo, and the woman he's hired to pursue. The woman is supposed to be Madeleine, the heiress who married his college friend Gavin Elster. Elster hires the detective to tail her, and in a monologue cut from the movie says that when he brought her to San Francisco, "She was like a child come home. Everything about the city excited her; she had to walk all the hills, explore the edge of the ocean, see all the old houses and wander the old streets; and when she came upon something unchanged, something that was as it had been, her delight was so strong, so fiercely possessive! These things were hers. And yet she had never been here before. . . . She possessed it," he says of her relationship to the city. "And then one day she changed again . . . and a great sigh settled on her, and the cloud came into her eyes. I don't know what happened that day, where she went, what she saw, what she did. But on that day, the search was ended. She had found what she was looking for. She had come home. And something in the city possessed her." She is supposed to be haunted by her Latina ancestress who died forlorn and mad, the betrayed mistress of a wealthy San Francisco man. The Madeleine in the movie wears a pale gray suit, has hair so blond it's almost white, drives a green Jaguar, is cool, mysterious, an elusive vision for the detective to follow.

And he follows her to the foot of the Golden Gate Bridge where she throws herself into the waves, to the California Palace of the Legion of Honor out at Land's End in the city's wild northwest, to the overgrown little cemetery at Mission Dolores, up and down the streets of downtown, so that the plot is a fiction but the film is an evocation of real places, all familiar ones to me, though here seen before I was born. He goes with her to a redwood forest where one of those crosscut redwood logs becomes a map of deep time—she points to tree rings from the nineteenth century and says, "Here I was born" and "here I died." Finally they go to another outlying mission where she leaps to her death from the bell tower before he, afflicted with vertigo, can follow her up the stairs. While recovering from his subsequent breakdown, he meets a brassy salesgirl from the elegant Magnin's department store downtown and, struck by her resemblance to Madeleine, dates her, dresses rather than undresses her, and forces her to come closer and closer to becoming Madeleine. Torn between love and judgment, she gives in. Finally, when Judy has the same pale hair, the same gray suit as the first woman he had followed and recklessly puts on a necklace that woman owned, he realizes that she was Madeleine, or rather that Madeleine never existed, that he had fallen in love with a scheme to cover up the murder of the real Mrs. Elster who was pushed from the tower that he, with his vertigo, could not ascend. The plot was concocted by Elster when the salesgirl was his mistress, but she was discarded afterward and is being discarded in another way by the detective determined she become someone else, someone dead. When he realizes the ruse, he forces her to return to the railless bell tower platform where Mrs. Elster was pushed to her death and, startled by a shadowy nun come up behind them, she backs up and is dead again.

Vertigo is an intricate tragedy, sometimes compared to Shakespeare, though it might be closer to *The Great Gatsby,* for part of the detective's desire is for her apparent aristocracy, her cool-colored evasion that he follows to the edge of death, the unreachable that for Gatsby is the green light at the end of Daisy's dock and for Gatsby's author is the irrecoverable past, the orgiastic future, the famous fresh green breast of the continent itself. There are Parisian novels in which love of a woman and love of the city become the same passion, though a lonely one in which wandering, stalking, haunting are consummation, and real communion is unimaginable. The same might be true of *Vertigo,* that Madeleine becomes what one of San Francisco's bad poets once called "the cool gray city of love," but neither hero nor heroine seems to much notice the places the camera caresses and probes. Told from the man's point of view, *Vertigo* is awash with romantic fog, but from the woman's perspective, it's about being forced to disappear—not from the top of a tower, but in everyday life as two successive lovers make her into someone else for their own ends, a common enough tragedy.

Most crabs come complete with their own shells, but the asymmetrical bodies of hermit crabs are usually described as soft and vulnerable. They take up residence in the shells of snails, whelks, periwinkles, and other hard-shelled creatures, and their body curves within the new home, a set of internal limbs holding onto the shell while big external claws find food and defend the crab from the outside world. The hermit crab: grabbing on one side and clinging on the other. Eventually the creature outgrows the shell, and thus comes the risky moment called the molt, when the crab is between shells. Sometimes it investigates a new shell before it molts and if the shell doesn't fit, slips back into the old one; sometimes it chases another crab out of a good-looking shell or eats a dead creature to empty out its shell. They are scavengers crawling the floor of the sea. Male hermit crabs often drag a female around by her claw, fighting off rival suitors, until she molts. Only when she is between shells can they mate. Their tiny young are borne along on the current until they reach a stage when they drop to the ocean floor and must quickly find a shell for protection, and thus begin adult life. Many love stories are like the shells of hermit crabs, though others are more like chambered nautiluses, whose architecture grows with the inhabitant and whose abandoned smaller chambers are lighter than water and let them float in the sea. *VPW*

I had seen *Vertigo* on the big screen again a year or so earlier, and one scene captivated me. In the first scene, the detective almost falls to his death, the incident from which he derives his vertigo; in the second he's at the home of an old friend. She lives in an apartment with drawings and paintings hung everywhere but the windows opening out onto sweeping views of the city below, makes her living drawing lingerie, and calls him Johnny while everyone else calls him Scottie. While he lounges, she chats with him and sketches a "revolutionary uplift" bra designed "on the principle of the cantilevered bridge": body as a vertiginous landscape, breasts a Golden Gate Bridge to jump from. Midge has hair almost as blond as Madeleine's, though big glasses, a sensible bob, and her nickname ensure she won't seem seductive. But her voice is like vanilla ice cream and when the detective complains about the corset he wears for his injured back and wonders whether many men wear them, she replies smoothly, "Quite a few." He sits upright and demands, "Do you know that from personal experience?" and she laughs and changes the subject.

Though she's full of what the French call *jouissance,* an erotic joy, she doesn't exist in the French novel from which *Vertigo* was adapted. An American screenwriter made her up. Most who write about the film seem to forget that it's she who broke off her engagement with the detective, as that initial scene reveals, and the screenwriters and director themselves seem to forget it in later passages when she becomes a far more conventional character with a sad, defeated devotion to Scottie. E. M. Forster wrote that novels have round and flat characters, and the flat ones are usually the minor figures, but *Vertigo* is a film with a paper doll Tristan and Iseult sliding across the foreground and this round figure making one startling appearance. She is an invitation to go in another direction than the tragic one of the film, for though the movie is in love with San Francisco, she is the only character who really seems immersed in the city's possibilities, and though the protagonists are driven in pursuit of pleasure and satisfaction, she seems to live amidst them. I began to tell myself a story—a novel if I wrote it down—about Midge.

When I was nineteen I wrote a play, badly. A woman hired a detective to find her vanished mate, and all the scenes took place in her room. The detective, through his investigations and conversations with her, comes to believe at various points that the missing man never existed, because she's mad or because she's invented the story to seduce him, or that he himself is one way or another that man and is mad himself. "Lost and Found," I called it. It was about yearning, about deception, about how she used the tale of having lost something to find something or to define something. Other fictions ran through my head at various times, and I would elaborate on some stories and characters for years, but they weren't what I was here for. Nonfiction seems to me photographic; it poses the same challenge of finding form and pattern in the stuff already out there and the same ethical obligations to the subject. Fiction like painting lets you start with a blank canvas, though as I began to turn this version of *Vertigo* into a story I called "Slip," I remembered what kind of truth fiction has: of the universal principles and the telling details, the minutiae that can add up to stories if you build characters around them. (In essays, ideas are the protagonists, and they often develop much like characters down to the surprise denouement.) In "Slip," Midge was just a childhood nickname for a woman called Margaretta and the detective a childhood sweetheart she outgrew.

She moved through a city I knew already, the city of the San Francisco Beat poets and artists who were the subject of my first book, and whose *annus miraculis* was 1957, the year *Vertigo* was made, years before I was born. Hitchcock's was a portrait of a closed world, a sort of Freudian strait of blind yearning, but the city was wide open with other possibilities at the time, the first flush of an era of hallucinogenic drugs, esoteric spiritual traditions, experimental film, a wilder, freer

A Field Guide to Getting Lost

poetry meant to be spoken aloud, collage and assemblage art made from the very rubble of the old houses being pulled down, engagement with the mystery of everyday life and sometimes with politics—people building up communities in which it might be possible to make another culture, another art, another era. Margaretta seemed to come into the movie out of this other world, and it's she who knows the owner of the antiquarian Argosy Bookstore who can tell the detective the history of the city. City with the Buddha Bar and the bar called Li Po in Chinatown, where the streetlights have oxidized bronze dragons curling up them, with the alleys south of Market named after nineteenth-century prostitutes and the houses sinking down because of soft ground and earthquakes, so their lintels are level with your eyebrows, with all the crests of all the hills that lift you out of the urban grid to see the ocean, the bay, and the hills across the water, with the evening fog tumbling over itself eastward past the streetlights, with in those days the jazz on Fillmore and the decrepit amusement park with its fun house and *musée mécanique* and hall of mirrors out at Land's End, near the Cliff House and Seal Rocks that show up in so many old photographs, this city edged in by wildness and opened up by imagination, whose poetry moves through that movie.

Of course there had to be a plot and a new center of gravity for a story with her at the center rather than the periphery, and *Vertigo* gradually faded into background for this other story. She told it backward, from her position as a painter with a daughter sometime in the 1960s, back to her childhood growing up with the detective the boy next door on the San Francisco peninsula when it was the Valley of Heart's Delight, huge orchards and small towns, not yet Silicon Valley. Slip, her prim mother telling her that a slip is something no one sees you wearing but that changes the appearance of what everyone sees, satin slips with the hedgerow landscapes of flowers and leaves in the lace next to the skin. Slip, the lingerie she drew as architecture, as the equivalent of drawbridges and gates and walls in that great age of girdles and foundations and garters and corsets, and a defloratory love scene where she was shocked not at his nakedness but her own overprinted with all the marks those straps and seams and buckles leave in soft flesh, the ghosts of garments. Slip, Judy a lingerie model as well as a salesgirl at Magnin's and Margaretta crossing paths with her in the course of drawing that lingerie while Judy talked on about herself, Judy letting slip what kind of an affair she was having and with whom and the decision Margaretta made to stay out of it that might have been the wrong decision. Slip, small drawings, paintings, letters, telegrams, receipts, and postcards falling out of the pages of a consignment of books at Argosy Bookstore, an autobiography inserted as page markers into those books, and Margaretta tracing them for the owner to the nephew of the estate they had come from. Slip, the painter whose career had trickled away during his internment in a prison camp for Japanese-Americans in the Second

World War and the paintings that included the landscape of the camps and the Sierra. The nephew became her companion in exploring the possibilities, a poet editing copy at the *Chronicle* while she was a painter drawing lingerie for a downtown department store, two people slipping from their original vocations into the dressing up of words and bodies. Slipping in, slipping out, slippery.

There are people for whom there is only one sun in the sky or darkness, and there are those who live in a night filled with stars, was her opening line, more or less. In a bar telling a ranger she was having an affair with, *As for nature, I am in love with the elemental forces, with fire and water, with gravity and evaporation and the properties of light, and there's as much of that in the city. It's in the way cream curls down into ice coffee and cigarette smoke coils up and the ice cubes in this drink are melting. I remember swinging in the backyard when I was a girl and scaring Johnny who lived next door and was just enough older to think he could supervise me, jumping off at the crest of the arc and coming down with my skirt billowing like a parachute.* She seemed to take pleasure in everything, to have a diffuse sensuality spread throughout the tangible world, in marked contrast to the protagonists chasing a conventional notion of satisfaction forever postponed. And so I gave her gravity, that sensation children pursue relentlessly, again and again, swinging, spinning, cracking the whip. I remember a motorcyclist telling me about the infinitely subtle ways racers use their bodies to turn at high speeds and the incredible pleasure of those acts. Gravity is about motion, weight, resistance, force, the most primary experience after all the touches on our skin, of being corporeal. And so it may be that gravity is a sweet taste of mortality and our strength to resist it, a luxuriating in the pull of the earth and the pull of muscles against it, in the momentum the two create, and in how close you can cut it, just as sex for women has the twin possibilities of procreation and annihilation.

The movie is about fear of gravity and ascent; I made both pleasures for her. She lived on the upswing as everything in *Vertigo* was falling. Mostly I gave her set pieces about the sensory world, and it's those I recall. *As for the grid of this city, the orchards on the peninsula had already taught me the pleasures of geometry, of the way you moved so that the diagonal lines through the plum trees disappeared and were replaced a minute later by the straight ones, and when you drove by, each avenue flashed by in a moment before the next one emerged from the crowd of trees, and I loved the way you could see the near trees swing by much faster than the far trees, as though you were on the outside edge of a circle rather than at the center, as though the center of the world was always near, but you swung on its periphery like a fly on a turning record, even though the road was straight. Perspective lessons, like in drawing class, though that's not a rule they taught us.* And of a man later, *I don't remember his face but every man who touched me made one gesture that never quite came to an end; I can feel the forearm of one across my belly as he swam up behind me in a lake, the rough kiss of*

148

A

Field

Guide

to

Getting

Lost

another on my palm, and sometimes I think that there might be some device like the X-ray machines they use to look at your feet in the shoe stores that would make these indelible impressions visible, a series of marks, the opposite of bruises, across and around me, and I went through the world dressed in those experiences, we all do.

There's not much more I remember of this book that seemed so complete in my head at one time, though I couldn't bring myself to write one word down, not wanting to start unless I could finish. Plot, character, dialogue seem mostly to have vanished as anything more than broad outlines. I know she and the editor wandered the city and its bars, went to the artists' parties, argued about vocations, and finally went into the mountains. The culminating excursion began as his desire to recover the poems he had buried in a tin at Manzanar, the bleak Second World War prison camp in the eastern Sierra for Japanese-Americans with the wonderful view of the highest peaks. By the time they arrived, though, he had recognized that his vocation wasn't going to be buried in the past. A couple of mountaineers they had met in a Big Pine diner invited them to go up nearby Mount Whitney with them, the highest point on the continent between Mexico and Canada, and they pulled out of Manzanar to take up the invitation at the last minute.

Tiresias's strange destiny began when he saw two snakes making love in the wilderness. He struck them and was turned into a woman as a result. Seven years later he came upon another pair of coupling snakes and struck them again to regain his manhood. Because he had been both a man and a woman, the gods asked him to settle an argument about which gender derives more pleasure from making love, and when he declared in favor of women, the annoyed Hera blinded him. As compensation, Zeus gave him the power of seeing the future, and he became a famous prophet. Or, in another story, he was struck blind for seeing Athena bathing, but in apology she took the snake from her breastplate and had it clean his ears with its tongue, so that Tiresias would understand the language of prophetic birds. It's Tiresias who tells Oedipus what crimes he has committed and is committing, who brings that cycle to its end with Oedipus's blinding and exile, and it's *Oedipus Rex* where he makes his main appearance. This prophet who sees despite his blindness, while Oedipus is only unseeing, blind or not, is much more interesting than Oedipus, whose world closes around him claustrophobically so that the stranger he kills is his father, the queen he marries is his mother. Tiresias's story isn't a tragedy, a knot of character untied only by death and exile, but a romance traveling through a terrain with the amplitude to include animals, gods, strangers, transformations. The word *romance* once meant this kind of questing journey—"usu. heroic, adventurous, or mysterious," says my dictionary. This older meaning suggests that romances in the other sense—"(3): a love story"—too should move through place and desire. Comedy, said Aristotle, ends in marriage, but since marriage is something other than an end, romance in one sense or both is what continues on afterward or it too lapses into tragedy. Margaretta— even Midge, unmodified—is the Tiresias of *Vertigo*.

I sent them up Mount Whitney, but what did they see? I hadn't been up the mountain at that point. I have since. Going the usual way, you walk up from a road high on the eastern side of the slope. The view to the east, behind you as you toil uphill, gets bigger and bigger. Around ten thousand feet you look across the wide valley between the Sierra and the first range of the White Mountains. When you've risen for an hour or more, you see over the range to the next one, and the desert landscape keeps getting larger and larger, until you're looking across basin after range after basin into the distant depths of Nevada. You realize that no matter how much terrain you cover there's far more than you ever will. Mountaineering is always spoken of as though summiting is conquest, but as you get higher, the world gets bigger, and you feel smaller in proportion to it, overwhelmed and liberated by how much space is around you, how much room to wander, how much unknown. All day you have been toiling uphill looking into the slope, on trail, switchback, in pine groves and above them, and the view behind you has gradually enlarged to the north, the south, the east. Sometimes birds, trees, the rocks underfoot draw your attention to the nearby, sometimes you are looking straight into the steepness ahead, but a turn or a pause lets you see the vastness in those three directions again, an infinite cloak of air wrapped around your back as you proceed. Finally, about thirteen thousand feet above the sea, you reach not the summit, which isn't so dramatic a change, but the crest. Whitney is only the highest point of a long ridge. As you step up to the ridgeline, the world to the west suddenly appears before you, a colossal expanse even more wild and remote than the east, a surprise, a gift, a revelation. The world doubles in size. Something like that happens when you really see someone, and if that's so then it has something to do with why everyone in *Vertigo* keeps falling. There wasn't any falling, any tragedy, at the center of "Slip," just moving on into this vastness.

The

Blue

of

Distance

When I think of the artist Yves Klein, I think of those absolutists who preceded him by a generation or two, those who vanished, think of the boxer and Dadaist poet Arthur Cravan who in 1918 was supposed to leave Mexico to meet his new wife in Argentina but was never seen again; of Everett Ruess, the bohemian who might have become an artist or writer had he not disappeared into the canyons of Utah at the age of twenty in 1934, leaving behind a final signature carved into the rock: "Nemo" or "no one"; of the aviator Amelia Earhart who disappeared over the Pacific in 1937; of the pilot Antoine de Saint Exupéry who left behind several lapidary books before his plane too disappeared, in 1944, in the Mediterranean. They were all saddled with a desire to appear in the world and a desire to go as far as possible that was a will to disappear from it. In the ambition was a desire to make over the world as it should be; but in the disappearances was the desire to live as though it had been made over, to refashion oneself into a hero who disappeared not only into the sky, the sea, the wilderness, but into a conception of self, into legend, into the heights of possibility.

Klein, who was beset with the most grandiose ambitions and the most mystical tendencies, who at twenty claimed to have signed the sky as his own work of art, who was obsessed with flight, levitation, and immateriality as well as the sky and the color blue that signified it, loved the legend of the Holy Grail, another story of disappearance, since those knights on the quest for the Grail who are pure enough to enter its presence do not return. It is only the sinners, the imperfect, the incompletely transformed, who come back bearing tales. Yves Klein was born to artist parents in the South of France in 1928, though his bourgeois Aunt Rose did more to raise him than these impecunious, unsettled painters, and it was this aunt who funded so many of his ventures. When he was still a baby, she and her mother consecrated him to the care of Saint Rita of Cascia, the patron saint of lost causes, and Klein himself, who managed to reconcile being an avant-gardist and a medieval mystic, made four pilgrimages to the saint's shrine in Italy as an adult. Or at least as a fully grown man, for he seems never to have stopped being a child in some ways, spoiled, petulant, impatient with restrictions, but also festive, generous, playful, and imaginative.

His two great influences arrived in his life the year he turned nineteen. One was the *Cosmogonie,* the bible of the Rosicrucian Order, by Max Heindel, which he read again and again over the next decade. For the next three or four years, Klein received weekly lessons by mail from the Rosicrucian Society in Oceanside, California. In the chaos of war and their own itinerant lives, his parents had allowed him to slip out of school at an early age, and his fascination with this one book seems to have in it something of the insularity of the underexposed who can be struck so forcefully by one source, one version. A mystical Christian sect with medieval roots, Rosicrucianism depicted the world in utopian and alchemical terms. Form and matter were, in Heindel's view, limitations and obstacles to the freedom and the unity of pure spirit, and Klein would make an art that embodied formlessness and the immaterial. That first year of Rosicrucian study, in which he was joined by his friends Claude Pascal and Armand Fernandez (who would become well-known as the artist Arman), the young men attempted to establish an ascetic life for themselves, meditating, fasting, turning vegetarian, though they also listened to jazz, jitterbugged (one picture shows a baby-faced Klein swinging a girl above his shoulders), and occasionally violated their vows of chastity. One day they divided the world between them: in one account, Arman was to have animals, Pascal the realm of plants, and Klein claimed the sky. In imagination he had traveled to the far side of the sky, "the side with no birds, no planes, no clouds, only pure and irreducible Space," the art critic Thomas McEvilley writes, and signed it. His ambition too was boundless.

The other great influence was judo, in which he began to train in the same year. He had a talent for it, and the way Asian martial arts imparted both mystical discipline and warriors' powers suited him. Perhaps too something about the way judo teaches its practitioners to fly through the air and land without harm and to transport others thus enchanted him. For some years, he conceived of judo as the arena in which he would become supreme, and he dreamed of riding a horse across Asia to Japan to study the art. As it turned out, though he spent three months in Ireland learning to work with and ride horses, he took a ship—paid for by his aunt—for Japan. Funded by Aunt Rose, he spent fifteen months there, and though he had begun to make small monochrome paintings and exhibited his own work as well as that of his parents, he focused more and more on judo. He wanted to become a fourth *dan* black belt, a level of mastery few in Europe had then achieved, win the European championship, and dominate the French judo federation. He worked intensely, enhancing his energy with the amphetamines that were still legal in Japan and France, and the drug seems to have become part of who he would be for the rest of his life: restless, energetic, insomniac, prolific, unpredictable, and grandiose. Through talent, enormous effort, and a little manipulation, he succeeded in being given the title of fourth *dan* black belt and took a boat back to France, but there his ambitions did not bear the fruit he imagined (and this is the last sense of lost: losing a competition, as in the Giants lost the Series). And thus began his artistic career.

This career, however, he began at a sort of pinnacle. The work he made required little technical skill but a brilliant grasp of ideas and of the art world, and these he had already. The Rosicrucians taught a doctrine of color, and Klein adapted this idea of pure realms of

color and color as a spiritual realm to begin his mono-
chromes. Though he initially painted canvases orange
as well as blue and eventually settled on a trinity of gold
leaf, a rich pink, and intense blue, it was the blue that
was to preoccupy and define him, the blue of the great
majority of his painterly works. Blue the color that represents the spirit, the sky, and water, the immaterial
and the remote, so that however tactile and close-up it
is, it is always about distance and disembodiment. By
1957, he was using only this color, a pure ultramarine
pigment mixed with a synthetic resin that would not,
like most painterly mediums, dilute it's deep, vibrant
intensity.

This formula he eventually patented as IKB, Interna-
tional Klein Blue (and he recognized and celebrated the
monomania of hundreds of paintings of the same color,
writing a symphony that consisted of one note and relat-
ing a parable of a flute player who for years played only
one note—but the right one, the beautiful one, the one
that opened up the mysteries). "With this blue," writes
one critic, "Klein at last felt able to lend artistic expression to his personal sense of life, as an autonomous realm
whose twin poles were infinite distance and immediate
presence." He claimed his blue work heralded the beginning of *l'époque bleu,* the Blue Age, and his first significant show bore this title. Held in Milan in 1957, it
featured eleven blue paintings, each featureless, each the
same size, each with a different price—thus the work
operated in the empyrean realm of ideas and as subver-
sion within the world of commerce. When the same

show was held in Paris, a thousand and one blue balloons were released into the evening sky.

The blue paintings were both objects that could be made and sold and windows into the boundless realms of the spirit. But there were more direct ways to reach that realm. For his second Parisian show, *Le Vide* (The Void), he purged the small gallery of everything it had contained and cleaned it thoroughly. After paying his first visit to Saint Rita's shrine—"I think this exhibition of the Void is rather dangerous"—he had painted the gallery pure white over a two-day period while mentally summoning immaterial forces. These he described as "a palpable pictorial state in the limits of a picture gallery. In other words, creation of an ambience, a genuine pictorial climate, and therefore, an invisible one. This invisible pictorial state within the gallery space should be so present and endowed with autonomous life that it should literally be what has hitherto been regarded as the best overall definition of painting: 'radiance.'" Two or three thousand people attended; members of the Garde République, who normally guarded only high dignitaries, were stationed at the entry; the police and firemen came because of the crowd; it was a hugely successful event, though what viewers thought they were seeing in the empty gallery remains open to question: Albert Camus wrote in the guest book, "with the void, full powers," punning on emptiness and fullness. The blue dye in the cocktails served at *Le Vide* caused all the drinkers to piss blue for days afterward.

He sold two immaterial pictures at this exhibition and later developed a formal transaction for selling access to the immaterial: the price for a *Zone of Immaterial Pictorial Sensibility* was paid in gold, half of which he immediately threw into a river, the ocean, "or in someplace in nature where this gold cannot be retrieved by anyone" to return it to life. To complete the ritual of disappearance and letting go, the buyers were obliged to burn the receipt filled out with his name and all the details of the purchase, so that they ended up with precisely nothing. Several *Zones* were sold. His work anticipated many of the concepts and gestures of art movements yet to be born, of conceptualists, minimalists, performance artists, and the Fluxus movement. His *Leap into the Void* of 1960, in some ways the culmination of all his work, was in many ways the most typical, since it combined the most sublime gesture of transcendence with prank, stunt, and self-promotion.

A plate of Waldseemüller's 1513 atlas depicts the central Atlantic, Spain, and the western bulge of Africa recognizably, but the upper right-hand shoulder of South America is nothing but a coastline full of small names and mouths of rivers and, in far bolder letters, across what is now Venezuela and Brazil, "Terra Incognita," unknown land. The phrase was common on old maps—even a 1900 atlas of mine marks out a part of the Amazon as "unexplored"—and is seldom found now. Between words is silence, around ink whiteness, behind every map's information is what's left out, the unmapped and unmappable. One of those in-depth local or state atlases that map ethnicity and education and principal crops and percentage foreign-born makes it clear that any place can be mapped infinite ways, that maps are deeply selective. A new map of the city of Las Vegas appears every month, because the place grows so fast that delivery people need constant updates on the streets, and this too is a reminder that maps cannot be commensurate with their subject, that even a map accurate down to blades of grass would fall out of accuracy as soon as the grass was grazed or trampled. The Great Salt Lake cannot be mapped with any degree of accuracy, because it lies in a shallow basin without drainage: any slight change in water level becomes an extensive change in shoreline.

Jorge Luis Borges wrote a parable about some cartographers who eventually created a map that was 1:1 scale and covered much of a nameless empire. Even at 1:1 scale, the two-dimensional map would be inadequate to depict the layers of being of a place, its many versions. Thus the map of languages spoken and the map of soil types canvas the same area differently, just as Freudianism and shamanism describe the same psyche differently. No representation is complete. Borges has a less-well-known story in which a poet so perfectly describes the emperor's vast and intricate palace that the emperor becomes enraged and regards him as a thief. In another version the palace disappears when the poem replaces it. The descriptive poem is a perfect map, the map that is the territory, and the story recalls another old one about a captive painter who at the Chinese emperor's dictate paints so wonderful a landscape that he is able to escape into its depths. These parables say that representation is always partial, else it would not be representation, but some kind of haunting double. But the terra incognita spaces on maps say that knowledge also is an island surrounded by oceans of the unknown. They signify that the cartographers knew they did not know, and awareness of ignorance is not just ignorance; it's awareness of knowledge's limits.

The eighteenth-century mapmaker Jean Baptiste Bourguignon d'Anville pronounced, "To destroy false notions, without even going any further, is one of the ways to advance knowledge." To acknowledge the unknown is part of knowledge, and the unknown is visible as terra incognita but invisible as selection—the map showing agricultural lands and principal cities does not show earthquake faults and aquifers, and vice versa. About a hundred and fifty years after Christ, a Roman named Crates made a globe based on the theory that the earth had four continents, three of them unknown. Around the same time Ptolemy drew up the atlas that was for a millennium and a half the standard source on the geography of the world. Says one map historian, "Ptolemy departed from the standard Greek conception of the inhabited world. He abandoned the idea of a world encompassed by water (in the restricted sense employed by Homer), of a circumfluent 'oceanus' relatively close by. Instead, he recognized the possibility and probability of Terra Incognita beyond the limits of his arbitrary boundary lines. In other words, he left the matter open to further investigation." Before Crates and Ptolemy, maps depicted a known world surrounded by water, and the complacency that must have gone with this sense that the world was, as the navigational term has it, encompassed must be our smugness now that maps of earth are so unlikely to say "Terra Incognita."

On Sebastian Cabot's 1544 map of the Americas, the whole of South America is drawn in, and so is Central America and the eastern coast. It's a beautiful map in the mode of the time: dark people as tall as provinces walk across the southern continent, a pair of white bears far larger than Cuba and Haiti walk in the opposite direction, west, across the northern continent, and clumps of grass that would dwarf mountain ranges dot the landmasses. But the west coast begins to dissolve where California starts. Beyond Baja California the line simply stops as though the world there was not yet made, as though it were neither land nor water, as though the Creator had not yet finished this part of earth, as though substance and certainty together dissolved there, and the phrase "Terra Incognita" spreads across this unmarked expanse. On a map drawn up by Gastaldi two years later, Asia is fit like a puzzle piece into the blankness of the North American west, so that it looks as though you could walk from Tibet to Nevada (which is not yet named or marked) without any detour to the north. Strange woolly shapes like caterpillars or clouds dot the continent, and more clouds boil off the edge of the round earth. The Pacific proper appears on later maps, but a mythical island of Java sometimes appears on it, far larger than the island that would finally be saddled with the name. Brazil, the Amazon, and California are also real places named after imaginary ones. In that Pacific, California was long portrayed as a huge island just off the west coast of North America, and the northwest coast of that continent remained undrawn, one of the last expanses of Terra Incognita to the Europeans mapping the world.

To imagine that you know, to populate the unknown with projections, is very different from knowing that you don't, and the old maps depict both states of mind, the Shangri-las and terra incognitas, the unknown northwest coast and the imagined island of California (whose west coast was nevertheless drawn in with some accurate details and names). When someone doesn't show up, the people who wait sometimes tell stories about what might have happened and come to half believe the desertion, the abduction, the accident. Worry is a way to pretend that you have knowledge or control over what you don't—and it surprises me, even in myself, how much we prefer ugly scenarios to the pure unknown. Perhaps fantasy is what you fill up maps with rather than saying that they too contain the unknown.

In ancient Greece, Herodotus spoke of the Atarantes in the African desert, a tribe who did without names, without meat, and without dreams, and reported that eastern Libya (as northwestern Africa was then called) sported "dog-headed men, headless men with eyes in their breasts (I don't vouch for this, but merely repeat what the Libyans say), wild men and women, and a great many other creatures by no means of a fabulous kind." Several centuries later, in the third century after Christ, Solinus located horse-footed men whose ears covered their bodies in place of clothes in Asia, birds that gave off light in Germany, and hyenas whose shadows stole the bark away from dogs in Africa. Even in 1570, Abraham Ortelius made a map of the world showing that grand imaginary continent, Terra Australis, giving it a River of Islands, a Land of Parrots, and other wholly fabricated features. Terra Australis was only definitively dispelled by Captain Cook's second expedition in 1772–75, just as the mythical Northwest Passage was done in by his final voyage. (Global warming may yet make it a reality.)

Into the nineteenth century, people continued to seek places that had been made up out of imagination and desire. It had already been discovered that the magical Cibola, whose name appears above New Mexico in the old maps, was only Kansas, that Paradise was not located in Central America as Columbus thought, once he admitted that the topographies he had bumped into were not Asia. But even in the 1840s John C. Fremont claimed to be looking for the Buenaventura River that led from the Great Salt Lake into the Pacific. A water route across or, as the long fantasy of the Northwest Passage had it, above the continent, was long desired and grudgingly abandoned, and the Donner Party died in part of a bad description of a shortcut across the salty western stretches of Utah in the uncharted region long called the Great American Desert. Long afterward, south-central Nevada remained unmapped and unexplored, one of the last parts of the lower forty-eight states to be filled in by surveyors, and into the early twentieth century it is strangely blank, though in 1900 the state was full of mining towns that no longer exist, Manse and Montgomery and Midas, Belleville and Reveille and Candelaria. Afterward, when a great swath of it the size of Wales became Nellis Air Force Base with the Nevada Test Site inside, the place where a thousand nuclear bombs like small incendiary suns were detonated over the decades, civilian maps often left the region entirely blank, as though it had gone back into the unknown.

The last map of California as an island was probably drawn up after Captain Cook's voyages, though the theory that the Sea of Cortez continued on up to rejoin with the Pacific, rather than being the strait that ends when Mexico's Baja California becomes the U.S.'s Alta California, had been dispelled earlier. Strange it is to look at the old maps of the world and see my part of the continent as island and a void: Nicholas d'Abbeville's 1650 map shows California as an island off a coast that becomes neither land nor water; Henrious Seile's 1652 map shades in more of the northwest coast, but refrains from drawing the sharp line of certainty. "Terra Borealis Incognita" say the block letters across a vast expanse. Even Pedro Font's 1777 map of the San Francisco Bay Area leaves the inland area north of the Golden Gate (as Fremont would later name it) blank, so that the territory of my childhood is terra incognita there.

During the buildup to the recent war on Iraq, whose two great central rivers come as close as anything on earth to the biblical paradise with four rivers flowing out of it, one of the vultures making the case for bombing Baghdad's civilians said, "There are known knowns. There are things we know we know. We also know there are known unknowns. That is to say, we know there are some things we do not know. But there are also unknown unknowns, the ones we don't know we don't know." This third category would prove crucial in the spasms and catastrophes of the war. And the philosopher Slavoj Zizek added that he had left out a fourth term, "the 'unknown knowns,' things we don't know that we know, which is precisely the Freudian unconscious, the 'knowledge that doesn't know itself,' as Lacan used to say," and he went on to say that "the real dangers are in the disavowed beliefs, suppositions, and obscene practices we pretend not to know about." The terra incognita spaces on maps say that knowledge too is an island surrounded by oceans of the unknown, but whether we are on land or water is another story.

In 1957, Yves Klein painted a globe his deep electric blue, and with this gesture it became a world without divisions between countries, between land and water, as though the earth itself had become sky, as though

looking down was looking up. In 1961, he began painting relief maps this same trademark blue, so that the
topography remained but the other distinctions vanished. Several of these maps depicted sections of France
but one showed Europe and northern Africa together.
Painted into one continuous mass, the distinctions vanished, even between Algeria and France, which were at
war at the time. "Klein used color," writes art historian
Nan Rosenthal, "as though it could be an explicit and
overtly political tool for ending wars." He had always
been against making distinctions and divisions, fulmi-
nating even against the line in painting and celebrating
the unifying force of color instead. And his work is a
reminder that, however beautiful, with their ships and
dragons, those old maps were tools of empire and capital. Science is how capitalism knows the world, a friend
remarks to me, and the distinctions and details these
maps marked out were first of all for merchants and
military expeditions. What was marked "Terra Incognita" was also what remained unvanquished. Painting
the world blue made it all terra incognita, indivisible
and unconquerable, a ferocious act of mysticism.

Throughout his work, Klein sought to transcend or
annihilate representation itself, which is always about
what is absent, for an art of immediacy and of presences,
even if it was the presence of the immaterial, the void.
He sought to erase the many for the sake of the one—
images for pure color, music for a single note, the material for the immaterial. His principal paintings were
without subject, and even those artworks showing the

human figure were traces of contact—the plaster on the male body, the paint on the female body—rather than representations. What was material was at least not representational, and he pursued dissolution, disappearance, and the dematerialized more directly with the exhibition *Le Vide,* with the flames that were, as gas jets, works of art themselves, or he scorched and pierced canvases to leave the mark of fire, with the gold thrown in the river, and with the *Leap into the Void.* Mystical because he was concerned with the dissolution of the rational mind, of expectation, of the industrial era, perhaps, and thus with erasing the map of reason and entering the void of pure consciousness that had been the subject of his first Paris exhibition.

The Leap into the Void of 1960 is a subject of some controversy. What remains of it is the official photograph. It shows a quiet Paris street with stone walls, an old sidewalk, leafy trees above the wall, and from the mansard roof of the wall or walled building on the left, Klein leaping. Not falling, but leaping upward, his body arced, his hands out, a few bits of hair flying up from his forehead, far above the street below, a dozen feet at least, leaping as though he need not even think of landing, as though he would never land, as though he were entering the weightless realm of space or the timeless realm of the photograph that would hold him up above the ground forever. The white sky of a black-and-white photograph, the dark suit—Klein was always impeccably dressed—and the upward curve of his back make it a formal and celebratory act, not just a

||||||

crisis of gravity. A train runs by in the background, a bicyclist pedals away down the right side of the otherwise abandoned street. Like Bruegel's painting of Icarus falling into the sea while a farmer plows, Klein was flying and no one seemed to know or care, or so says the photograph (which is, of course, evidence that at least photographers were present).

He published a single edition of a four-page newspaper, *Le Dimanche* (*Sunday*), whose front page was dominated by this photograph of the leap and whose various newspaper-formatted texts were a description of and manifesto for his work. "A Man in Space!" said the headline for the photograph, parodying the space race that sought to put a man into orbit, and a caption read, translated, "The Monochrome [Yves le Monochrome was his *nom de guerre*], who is also a fourth dan black belt judo champion, regularly practices dynamic levitation! (with or without a net, at the risk of his life). He means to be in shape to go into space soon to join his favorite work: an aerostatic sculpture composed of 1,001 blue balloons, which, in 1957, escaped from his exhibition into the sky over Saint-Germain-des-Pres never to return. To liberate sculpture from the base has been his preoccupation for a long time." The text is quintessentially Klein, a mix of astute engagement with artistic practice and contemporary events, good-humored prank, and mysticism. It continues, "Today anyone who paints space must actually go into space to paint, but he must get there without any faking, and neither in an airplane, a parachute, nor a rocket: he must go there by his own means, by an autonomous, individual force: in a word, he must be capable of levitating." Thus did the Rosicrucian and judo studies of his earlier years come to a culmination. "The Blue Revolution Continues," says a bold caption above the masthead.

Klein had been obsessed with flying for much of his life. Says Rotraut, his widow, "He was sure he could fly. He used to tell me that at one time monks knew how to levitate, and that he would get there too. It was an obsession. Like a little child he really was convinced that he could do it." Flying meant literally entering the sky he had claimed, meant vanishing, an obsession of his equal to his preoccupation with levitation, according to one close friend, and it meant entering the void. The leap into the void is sometimes read as a Buddhist phrase about enlightenment, about embracing the emptiness that is not lack as it seems to westerners, but letting go of the finite and material, embracing limitlessness, transcendence, freedom, enlightenment. "Come with me into the void!" wrote Klein, "You who like me, dream / Of that wonderful void / That absolute love. . . ."

A photograph is evidence, but this photograph of Klein's leap is evidence of something more complicated than a man beginning to fly, and the accounts vary wildly. The photograph is only the trace or souvenir of the work of art, which is the leap itself. Taken on October 19, 1960, it is one of the first of a new kind of photograph to become important in that decade, the photograph as document of an artwork that was too remote, too ephemeral, too personal to be seen otherwise, an artwork that could not be exhibited and would otherwise be lost, so the photograph stands in for it. Artists showed documentation of bodily acts, ephemeral gestures, manipulations of remote landscapes, so that the photograph wasn't there primarily as a work of art or aesthetic experience but a souvenir of the unseen, the past, the elsewhere, a tool for the imagination.

The photograph is a montage: Klein the judo master did indeed leap, but there was a tarpaulin held by ten judo practitioners below; so the photograph splices together Klein above and the street below without the tarp and colleagues. But McEvilley tells it another way. In his account, taken from those close to Klein, including those who witnessed the multiple leaps, there was a true leap into the void that January, but the principal witnesses were absent and there was no evidence. Bernadette Allain, the woman with whom he lived before Rotraut, witnessed the initial leap and recalls, "For a judoka who knew how to fall, it was not extraordinary. . . . It would be expected of someone at his level of training to know how to recover and fall. He did it as a challenge or act of defiance, to prove that he was capable of leaping into the void—that is not leaping out of a window, but leaping toward the sky. . . . He had nothing underneath him but the pavement—nothing!" The site of that leap was the gallerist Colette Allendy's house on Rue de l'Assomption, the street of the Assumption, which in Catholic France can mean nothing other than the bodily assumption of the Virgin Mary into heaven, particularly since this quiet street in the Sixteenth Arrondissement is only a few blocks from the Rue de l'Annonciation, the street of the Annunciation (off which I lived in a maid's room for several months when I was seventeen, I realize, looking at an old Paris map bemused to think that I must have passed the site of the leap many times without knowing it, that each of our lives traces its own map onto the shared terrain).

After the January leap, he went to visit a pilot friend of his who would indeed disappear for good into the void, in his airplane in the Himalayas; this was the last time Klein was to see him. One trace of the leap was Klein's limp from "a twisted ankle" for some time afterward. He found that few believed he had made the leap, and so he performed again for the cameras that October at another site. This was the time he leapt with a tarp, twice, for the cameras. Rotraut had persuaded him not to make another leap with nothing beneath him but the pavement. The official photograph shows him traveling upward with composure. Another one shows him blurrily facing downward and thrashing a bit, not like a man falling but perhaps like a cat falling. But in the public photograph, he soars upward forever, truly flying for the moment the camera preserved.

What else is there to tell of Yves Klein? The year after the three leaps he went to the United States where he met with a cold reception in New York and a warm

174

||||||

A
Field
Guide
to
Getting
Lost

one in Los Angeles, whose art scene was just beginning to burst into bloom. There he was eager to visit Death Valley, and a young artist and curator drove him out deep into the desert, though not all the way there, and somehow this journey to the far west from which his Rosicrucian lessons had come seemed to complete the journey begun with his journey to the far east to study judo. Afterward his mind turned more and more to death, which he had always associated with flying and disappearing. Back in Paris he began his planetary reliefs, the blue-painted relief maps, he married Rotraut, who was pregnant, and his heart, taxed by amphetamines, began to fail. He died in June of 1962, thirty-four years old, a few months before his son, also Yves Klein, was born. Though he was tragically young, his life looks like a meteor, a shooting star, a complete trajectory across the sky, a finished work of art.

Movies are made out of darkness as well as light; it is the surpassingly brief intervals of darkness between each luminous still image that make it possible to assemble the many images into one moving picture. Without that darkness, there would only be a blur. Which is to say that a full-length movie consists of half an hour or an hour of pure darkness that goes unseen. If you could add up all the darkness, you would find the audience in the theater gazing together at a deep imaginative night. It is the terra incognita of film, the dark continent on every map. In a similar way, a runner's every step is a leap, so that for a moment he or she is entirely off the ground. For those brief instants, shadows no longer spill out from their feet, like leaks, but hover below them like doubles, as they do with birds, whose shadows crawl below them, caressing the surface of the earth, growing and shrinking as their makers move nearer or farther from that surface. For my friends who run long distances, these tiny fragments of levitation add up to something considerable; by their own power they hover above the earth for many minutes, perhaps some significant portion of an hour or perhaps far more for the hundred-mile races. We fly; we dream in darkness; we devour heaven in bites too small to be measured.

A
Field
Guide
to
Getting
Lost

One-Story

House

I was carrying the tortoise in both hands, holding it out in front of me like an altar boy's Bible or a divining rod as I walked around the periphery of the room. Each plate of its ruddy shell was distinct. It leaked as I carried it. More water came forth than a tortoise that size could possibly store. The creature was a fountain, a cleft rock in my hands, and when I awoke I realized that the room in which I paced was my childhood bedroom.

I had been wandering through that house every now and again ever since I'd left it at age fourteen. A quarter century had passed, and I still wasn't out of it, in my dreams. It was a classic suburban house of its era, single-story, L-shaped. The houses children draw look like faces with upstairs windows for eyes and a door for a mouth. They have a solidity and a centrality that makes them home as the head is home. This house, with its public rooms that opened one into another as though they were only distended passageways and its bedrooms appendix-like cul-de-sacs, had no center, but my psyche was stuck in it. The previous owners' plantings all around it were strange, exotic, bottlebrush and artificial strawberry tree, a spruce the same powder blue as the corduroy pants boys wore then, succulents and other plants that were nameless, unrecognizable, inedible, with shiny leaves or spiky ones. One plant up a narrow side plot in perpetual shade bloomed annually with a single colossal lily that looked as though it were made of crumpled black leather from some thin-skinned creature. In front of each of the two children's bedrooms facing the street was a misshapen juniper, and at night the headlights of passing cars made the shadows of their branches whirl around the walls like pterodactyls. Awnings, eaves, and patio roof prevented sunlight from reaching in directly to this place made of formica and tile and linoleum and dark green wall-to-wall carpeting with a nap like aerial photographs of forests. Everything about it seemed to be made of chilly alien materials, and the swimming pool was strangest of all.

The pool was unheated, too cold for skinny kids to jump in most of the year, but it always needed sweeping and skimming to get the dirt and debris out, and the tools for doing that were fantastically long, like cutlery for a Behemoth with its head up in the clouds. It was the usual pale turquoise with a pink cement rim that abraded bare feet and the sharp smell of chlorine emanating from its waters. There's something fearful and mysterious about every body of water, murky water that promises unseen things in unseen depths, clear water that shows you the bottom far below as if you could fall into it, though the water would buoy you up in that strange space neither air nor ground. The term "a body of water" is apt, for here was a mysterious body thirty feet long, eight feet tall at the far end, a transparent captive into whose depths you could throw yourself. Even the lightest breeze patterned the water on the surface, and the sun turned those patterns into strange skeins of light that fled across the bottom, endless nets cast across a fishless sea. Afterward I dreamed over and over of the pool as well as the house. It was as though I couldn't find my way out of the house, as though I was still lost in it, but the pool was less part of the labyrinth than its holy well.

Terrible things happened in that house, though not particularly unusual or interesting ones; suffice to say there's a reason why therapists receive large hourly sums for listening to that kind of story. Or maybe there's one thing to say, about the capitalism of the heart, the belief that the essences of life too can be seized and hoarded, that you can corner the market on confidence, stage a hostile takeover of happiness. It's based on scarcity economics, the notion or perhaps the feeling that there's not enough to go around, and the belief that these intangible phenomena exist in a fixed quantity to be scrambled for, rather than that you can only increase them by giving them away. A story can be a gift like Ariadne's thread, or the labyrinth, or the labyrinth's ravening Minotaur; we navigate by stories, but sometimes we only escape by abandoning them.

Some years ago, I dreamed that my mother had fixed up the house, or had done so in dream terms, heavy-handed ones: the swimming pool was surrounded by broken glass, the bathroom had two sunken tubs shaped like coffins, and my own small bedroom had been brightly repainted with a line of dancing skeletons on one wall. I dreamed of my father every now and again too, and long after his death, not long after the hermit taught me to shoot, there was a period in which I told him to stand back because I was armed. After this series of victories, he became harmless. Clearly, I was getting somewhere over the years. I took over the master bedroom and decided to move, I drove the family out of my own room, and then came the dream of the tortoise.

In dreams, nothing is lost. Childhood homes, the dead, lost toys all appear with a vividness your waking mind could not achieve. Nothing is lost but you yourself, wanderer in a terrain where even the most familiar places aren't quite themselves and open onto the impossible. But the morning after I carried the leaking tortoise, I knew I was no longer stuck in the house. The weight of a dream is not in proportion to its size. Some dreams are made of fog, some of lace, some of lead. Some dreams seem to be made out of less the usual debris of the psyche than bolts of lightning sent from outside.

I wondered where the tortoise came from. I remembered riding a Galapagos tortoise in a zoo when I was two, remembered a box turtle my middle brother had

as a pet, and the small red slider turtles painted up for Easter back when animal cruelty standards were lower, read about how the Zuni think of turtles as the spirits of the dead returned, noticed that every image of turtles and tortoises had a sort of pull on me. Months passed before I remembered an encounter with a desert tortoise almost a decade earlier, when I was camping in the Mojave with a few other women. I saw the full-grown tortoise in the center of a secondary road near Death Valley and stopped my truck. We got out to look at it, and I recited what I knew: that it is bad to touch these creatures, because they are stressed by the transformation of their environment, vulnerable to illness and to infection, particularly to a respiratory disorder, and touching could contaminate them. In crisis, they sometimes void all their stored water, water slowly extracted from leaves and gulped up from puddles after hard rain, water that can make up to forty percent of their body weight, and losing their water is a crisis itself.

But they are also prone to being run over by cars and off-road vehicles throughout their territory, the Mojave and western Colorado deserts. We watched the tortoise, which had stopped when we did, watched a few approaching cars in the distance, and then I took out a clean dish towel and, with the dish towel between my hands and its shell, lifted the creature. It had retracted its head and limbs, and so I carried a heavy dust-colored dome with each plate etched in concentric lines, a mosaic of mandalas. Holding it before me, I strode about fifty feet into the scrubby desert and set it down facing in the direction it had been going. Put down, it walked again with an odd tipping motion, its shell lurching a little with each step. One of the most famous Buddhist tales is about a pair of monks sworn to keep apart from women. One day they come to the edge of a turbulent river. A woman there implores them to help her cross—old fables are short on athletic women—and one of them carries her through the waters. After the two monks have been walking for some time on the farther shore, the other monk reproaches him for breaking his vows. His companion replies, "Why are you still carrying her? I put her down on the far side of the river." Several years after that little encounter in the desert, I was still carrying the tortoise, but it had become a compass, a visa, an amulet.

The desert tortoise is in danger of extinction—it officially received "threatened" status from the U.S. Fish and Wildlife Service in 1990—because of human encroachments. The causes of its diminishing numbers are many. Nonnative plants have disrupted its diet, and grazing animals, dogs, vehicles, development, military bases have all had their impact, as has the widespread capturing of the creatures for pets. An increase in garbage dumps in the desert has vastly increased the raven population, and ravens prey on young tortoises during the five years or so before their shells harden sufficiently to protect them. (The hermit once found a young tortoise with severe pecking wounds in its shell; he brought it home and called in a zoo veterinarian he knew to try to save it with kitchen-sink surgery—I was away then, and he delivered telephone reports on "Miss Tortoise" for a few days, then told me that "Miss Tortoise didn't make it.") The desert tortoise can go for more than a year without food or water, hibernates several months a year in its colder northern reach, stays in its cool burrow during the hottest part of summer, seldom roams more than a mile from its burrow, walks slowly, lives slowly, to a great age, upward of a century.

||||||

They have existed for sixty million years or so. The plan to save them is designed to give them a fifty percent chance of existing in five hundred years. The government is unwilling to dedicate more resources or curtail more activities than make the odds even.

In 1919, a young ethnographer fell in love with a blacksmith from the Chemehuevi tribe whose large territory is the heart of tortoise habitat. The blacksmith, George Laird, was already forty-eight, and as a boy he had learned much lore that was being forgotten and lost and diluted. The winter he was sixteen—about 1888—he nursed a man in the agonizing last stages of syphilis, and the dying man taught the boy a purer form of their language and "filled the long, sleepless nights with tales of the Immortals, the pre-human Animals Who Were People, told with great style and elegance." During the twenty-one years the Chemehuevi man and the ethnographer, Carobeth Laird, were inseparable, she learned the language, the songs, and the stories he knew, and long after he died, when she herself was old, she turned her notes and memories into a book of ethnography. Of the tortoise, she recorded, "This reptile was desirable for food, but it also had a peculiar aura of sacredness. It was and is to this day symbolic of the spirit of the People. 'A Chemehuevi's heart is tough, like the turtle's.' This 'tough-heartedness' is equated with the will and the ability to endure and to survive." But the tortoise is not surviving us well.

It is in the nature of things to be lost and not otherwise. Think of how little has been salvaged from the compost of time of the hundreds of billions of dreams dreamt since the language to describe them emerged, how few names, how few wishes, how few languages even, how we don't know what tongues the people who erected the standing stones of Britain and Ireland spoke or what the stones meant, don't know much of the language of the Gabrielanos of Los Angeles or the Miwoks of Marin, don't know how or why they drew the giant pictures on the desert floor in Nazca, Peru, don't know much even about Shakespeare or Li Po. It is as though we make the exception the rule, believe that we should have rather than that we will generally lose. We should be able to find our way back again by the objects we dropped, like Hansel and Gretel in the forest, the objects reeling us back in time, undoing each loss, a road back from lost eyeglasses to lost toys and baby teeth. Instead, most of the objects form the secret constellations of our irrecoverable past, returning only in dreams where nothing but the dreamer is lost. They must still exist somewhere: pocket knives and plastic horses don't exactly compost, but who knows where they go in the great drifts of objects sifting through our world?

Once I found a locket with a crescent moon and star spelled out in rhinestones on one face, unreadably intricate initials on another, and two ancient photographs inside, and someone must have missed it terribly but no one claimed it, and I have it still. Another time, traveling down a river in one of the last great wildernesses, a roadless place the size of Portugal, I lost a sock early in the trip and a pair of sunglasses later, and I think of

186

||||||

A
Field
Guide
to
Getting
Lost

them littering that wilderness so clear of such clutter, there still or found by someone who might have wondered as I did about the woman with the locket. On that trip I leaned over the side of the raft and stared straight down for hours at the floor of that river whose name almost no one knows that flows into another little-known river, stared at thousands of stones, hundreds of thousands of millions of stones sliding by, gray, pink, black, gold, under the clearest water in the whole world, floating for miles and days on water I drank straight out of the river. Material objects witness everything and say nothing. Animals say more. And they are disappearing.

That things should be lost to our knowledge is one thing, in which we don't know where we are or they are; that things should be lost from the earth is another. There is a strange crossroads these days, between the actual and the known. Biologists estimate that about 1.7 million species are known, but that there are between 10 and 100 million on earth. Our discovery and categorization of species increases at a manic rate, but so does the disappearance of both known and unknown species. More is known; there is less to know; we lose both what we know and what we don't. It is certain that species are vanishing without ever having been known to science. To think about this is to imagine the space inside our heads expanding but the places outside shrinking, as though we were literally devouring them.

In dreams I have been an eagle and a green finch, have met a three-headed coyote, wolves, foxes, lynxes, dogs, lions, songbirds, fish, snakes, cattle, seals, many horses and cats, some who talk, a woman giving birth by cesarean to a full-grown stag that ran away, still wet with the juices of birth, down a dark, tree-shrouded road, a gazelle fawn that a woman breast-fed, a brown bear who married a woman. "They are all beasts of burden in a sense," Thoreau once remarked of animals, "made to carry some portion of our thoughts." Animals are the old language of the imagination; one of the ten thousand tragedies of their disappearance would be a silencing of this speech. A man once told me that much of my writing was about loss, that that was how I imagined the world, and I thought about that comment for a long time. In that sense of loss two streams mingled. One was the historian's yearning to hang onto everything, write everything down, to try to keep everything from slipping away, and the historian's joy in retrieving out of archives and interviews what was almost forgotten, almost out of reach forever. But the other stream is the common experience that too many things are vanishing without replacement in our time. At any given moment the sun is setting someplace on earth, and another day is slipping away largely undocumented as people slide into dreams that will seldom be remembered when they awaken. Only the continuation of abundance makes loss sustainable, makes it natural. There are more sunrises coming, but even dreams could be emptied out.

The golden age, the dreamtime, is the present, and too much in it is leaking out now. The Times Square clock that counted down to the millennium, its seconds, minutes, hours, days racing away on a digital display, could have been kept for endangered species, at least thirty lost a day, more than ten thousand a year, half of all of them to be gone in a century unless something changes radically, or everything does. Imagine the present as already a Noah's ark, and greed and development and poison as a trio of pirates marching the animals and plants over the edge, to the bottom of the sea that is the past. No more flocks of passenger pigeons darkening the midwestern sky for hours and days in the past century, all known Sampson's pearly mussels gone from midwestern rivers by the 1930s, no more Santa Barbara song sparrows since 1959, no more Tecopa pupfish since 1972, an estimated 142 Sonoran pronghorn left in the U.S. as of the late twentieth century but less than half that by 2002, seventy-two species of snail missing in Hawaii, the blue pike of the Great Lakes gone extinct right about when men first walked on the moon, the speckled cormorant gone from Alaska about the time of the gold rush.

During that California gold rush, Yankees in quantity first came through the heart of the desert tortoises' territory. The Death Valley Forty-Niners were in haste to make it to the goldfields of the Sierra Nevada, and because they had arrived in the Great Basin too late to go over the Sierra's snowy passes, they hired a Mormon guide to take them down the Spanish Trail to southern California. They called themselves the Sand Walking Company, a corruption of the San Joaquin Company, because none of them recognized the saint whose Spanish name had been given to a river and valley in the southern mother lode. A twenty-year-old New Yorker named O.K. Smith showed up on the trail with pleasant stories of a more direct route to central California, and most of the wagons switched over to the alleged shortcut. The guide continued on the Spanish Trail with the few who didn't. The strays were abetted by a map that government explorer John C. Fremont—"the pathfinder"—had drawn up, showing a long range running east-west that happened not to exist (a bad map had much to do with the Donner Party's 1846 stranding too). "These mountains are not explored, being only seen from elevated points on the northern exploring line," said the map, above an area marked in larger letters: "Unexplored." The Sand Walkers thought they could travel along the foothills of the fictitious mountain range. Many turned back when the terrain became impassible for wagons, and the rest broke up into smaller parties. These parties got stranded in Death Valley, the lowest land in the Western Hemisphere, a dry lake bed like an empty mouth between two sharp rows of mountain ranges.

"We had been in the region long enough to know that the higher mountains contained the most water, and that the valleys had bad water or none at all, so that while the lower altitude to the south gave some promise of easier crossing it gave us no promise of water or grass, without which we must certainly perish," wrote William Manly, half a century later. "In a certain sense we were lost. The clear nights and days furnished us with the means of telling the points of the compass as the sun rose and set, but not a sign of life in nature's wide domain had been seen for a month or more. A vest pocketful of powder and shot would last a good hunter until he starved to death, for there was not a liv- ing thing to shoot, great or small." Manly was a skilled hunter and outdoorsman, and there's no ready expla- nation for why the landscape through which he traveled in the winter of 1849–50 seemed to be so without wildlife. For these pioneers, the Mojave was an empty quarter, without water, without animals, without names, without maps, without all the things that give a place life and meaning. They were afraid of Indians, though the only two survivors of one party of eleven men made it because they were rescued by Paiutes. The skeletons of the other nine were found a decade later, inside a low circle of stones. Other parties were shown the location of precious waterholes, springs, and streams by Indians they encountered. Columbus had arrived in the Caribbean he mistook for the Indies almost four hundred years before, but there had been few direct disturbances of the indigenous inhabitants of the more remote western regions, and they were not yet resisting what was not yet a crisis.

One starving pioneer attempted to buy a biscuit off a neighbor for ten dollars and was refused. Another buried $2,500 to lighten his load, having been unable to find anyone who wanted to carry the gold coins for a half share of them. He was never able to find the burial spot either. Still others found ore that suggested rich mines, had they only the food and water to survive there. The

Lost Gunsight Mine, named after a silver-rich piece of ore that one of the Death Valley Forty-Niners had made into a gunsight, became famous, as did the Lost Goller Mine. The latter mine consisted of a few nuggets picked up by John Goller's companion. Upon seeing them, Goller snapped, "I want water; gold will do me no good." The mines themselves were legends later visitors would look for in vain, built out of bits of ore brought out by these desperadoes. It was a strange sojourn, this journey through a landscape where all their hopes of finding mineral wealth were set aside, where wealth meant nothing and water everything, where they were faced with critical decisions about sharing and surviving, where they all faced death and some met it. It was a detour into the essential and the introspective, as the desert often is, and they were lost in it.

The nomadic Chemehuevi navigated wide expanses of this arid terrain with songs. The songs gave the names of places in geographical order, and the place names were descriptive, evocative, so that a person who'd never been to a place might recognize it from the song. Carobeth Laird commented, "Nowadays when a song is sung it takes great leaps from one locality to another, because there is no one who remembers the route in its entirety." She explained further, "How does that song go?" meant "What is the route it travels?" Men inherited songs from their father or grandfather, and the song gave them hunting rights to the terrain it described. Despite Manly's experience, there seemed to be plenty to hunt for those who knew where to look, and when. The Salt Song describes the route of a flock made up of every sort of land bird in the region, and it "travels all night, arriving at Las Vegas about midnight, at Parker towards morning, and back home to the place of origin by sunrise. If the night on which it is sung is very short, the Salt Song—as the other hereditary songs—may be shortened so that it will not outlast the night." In that song the birds began to leave the flock toward morning, each dropping out into its own place in this orderly world of words and places. A song was the length of the night and a map of the world, and the arid terrain around Las Vegas was the Storied Land of the great myths. The Mojave people just to the south had a turtle song that also lasted the length of a night or several nights.

The silence in which Manly and a companion walked out of Death Valley to seek help for two families stranded there forms a strange contrast. They carried only small canteens and soon ran out of water. So they "traveled along for hours, never speaking, for we found it much better for our thirst to keep our mouths closed as much as possible, and prevent the evaporation." They were unable to eat the dried ox meat they carried because their mouths were too parched, and when they finally found a small sheet of ice like "window glass," they quenched their thirst only to find that they were ravenous. It took Manly and his companion twenty-three days to find help and return with provisions and a route out. By that time their traveling companions had despaired of the young men's ability and altruism, so they were surprised as well as rejoiced at their return. The whole party finally reached the settlements four months after they'd taken their shortcut. Afterward they returned to the mapped world and to their familiar way of living. "Every point of that terrible journey is indelibly fixed upon my memory, and though seventy-three years of age on April 6, 1893, I can locate every camp, and if strong enough, could follow that weary trail from Death Valley to Los Angeles with unerring accuracy," wrote Manly in his memoir *Death Valley in '49*, and it was his party who named the place where they were stuck Death Valley.

I know the Storied Land or the country a little north of it. It's the first desert I came to know and the place that taught me to write. In my late twenties, I started going to the Nevada Test Site, where a thousand nuclear bombs were detonated over the years, started going there with thousands of others to oppose the nuclear testing, a wild mix of Western Shoshones and pagans and Mormons and Franciscans and Buddhists and anarchists and Quakers. The place demanded to be described not with the straight line of a single story but with stories like the roads that converge upon a capital, for many histories had arrived there in the decades since the Death Valley Forty-Niners, and some of the old ones had not been forgotten. The people I met there invited me into a wider sense of home in the West, and a tortoise I picked up not so far from there would carry me out of my old home, a tortoise that might have been Turtle Island itself, the old name for the whole continent, as though the whole continent could be home, and perhaps it's this sense of place that sprung me from the house I left a quarter century before.

Six or seven blocks northwest of where I live now is the hill where the last Brown Satyr butterfly was collected in the 1870s, as that intensely local species was going extinct. Some of the individuals of the gold rush were likeable, but their cumulative effect was terrible; they worked feverishly to acquire what could be hoarded— notably the tons of gold dug out of the mountains—and for it they paid with what couldn't be hoarded and didn't belong to them, the clear streams and rivers filled up with miners' mercury and dirt, the salmon runs already starting to fail in their time, the forests chopped down for smelters, the California grizzly extinct everywhere but the state flag by 1922, the languages and stories of the tribes devastated by violence and by disease in this place that was blank and unborn to the miners. It was this acquisitiveness and its increasingly sophisticated new technologies that came to extract more and more wealth from the wild and remote places of the world to empty them out, filling up banks with more money than could ever be spent, more than there are things to buy. Now the scarcity is real, and growing.

It's not as simple as a morality tale because what came into being is partly beautiful, and it has come to have its own complexities. There's a Catholic university on the hill where the butterfly left off being, and I have heard great poets read there and environmentalists speak. About twice as far from my white birdcage of an apart-

One-Story
House

ment in the opposite direction is the San Francisco Zen Center, one of the key locations for the arrival of Buddhism in the West. The handsome brick building in a poor neighborhood was erected long ago as a residence for Jewish women, and a few Stars of David are still worked into the iron balconies. One morning four months after my midsummer dream of the tortoise, I woke up knowing it was time to go there. I arrived in time for the Saturday morning talk and sat behind a huge African-American man. Whenever he shifted his weight the altar appeared and it was the more interesting in glimpses. That day, someone mentioned that the stone Buddha on it was from an Afghanistan that had ceased to exist long ago. I had just given the two wool blankets I had inherited from that house in my dreams to the Quakers for winter relief in Afghanistan. The statue with its serene full face seemed to be looking back from the place where the blankets were going. Its soft brown stone spoke of an aridity and solidity that made the place real, made me see stony mountains shaped by erosion into folds like the curves of the statue's robes.

A gaunt man with cropped gray hair sat down cross-legged, arranged his dark robes, and without preamble began to tell a story, softly, slowly, with long pauses: "Good morning. For many years there was someone who used to come here and sell us boxes of candy. Actually they were tins of candy, and they were caramel-coated in chocolate, and they looked like little chocolate turtles. So we called him the Turtle Man, and the Turtle Man would come and sell us this very sweet caramel-covered chocolate. And the Turtle Man couldn't see. He was blind, so we bought two boxes instead of one. And then we'd put them in the desk in the office and then, even though we all thought they were way too sweet, we would eat them—quickly. The Turtle Man did this for many years. Like many blind people, he had a white cane, and he'd tap his way up the stairs and then he'd tap the door, and then he'd come in. We'd do our transaction, and then he'd leave.

"And one day I was out on the street right out here and I heard this voice go help . . . help . . . help . . . and it was the Turtle Man, and he was standing over there on the corner. He needed to cross the street and his way of crossing the street was to stand on the curb and say help and just say help until someone came along and helped him across the street. I didn't watch him, but I assume that at each street crossing this was how the Turtle Man negotiated the crossing: he just stood there and said help, help.

"So I thought, Isn't that really amazing? What an amazing life. You walk along and you reach a barrier and you stop and you just call out help. You don't know who you're talking to, you don't know who's around if anyone, and you wait, and then somebody turns up and they help you across that barrier, and then you walk on knowing that pretty soon you're going to meet another barrier and you're going to have to stop again and cry out help, help, help, not knowing if anyone's there, not knowing who it will be that will turn up to help you across the next barrier.

"And yet somehow the Turtle Man could roam around the city selling boxes of turtle candy, coming to places like Zen Center and persuading them to buy a couple of cans.

"And he was, you know, a bit of a hustler. He knew we didn't really want them, but he knew we were good for two cans. The Turtle Man wasn't a fool. It was always a kind of a thrill to see him. It was almost like it was a miracle. It was like the Turtle Man defied gravity, he defied common sense, he defied conventionality. It was like the Turtle Man was a superhero, so it was always a little bit exciting and a little bit joyous when he turned up at the door.

"How else could we break through the spell that we weave if we didn't have a little piece of Turtle Man in us? But this is a very dangerous proposition because most of us don't have the excellent training of Turtle Man. Turtle Man had no option. It was either stay in bed or get up and meet the impassable barrier and cry for help. Those were the options.

"Maybe if I really paid attention to my life I'd notice that I don't know what's going to happen this afternoon and I can't be fully confident that I'm competent to deal with it. Maybe we're willing to let in that thought. It has some reasonableness to it, I can't exactly know, but chances are, possibilities are, it's not going to be much different than what I've usually experienced and I'll do just fine, so we close up that unsettling possibility with a reasonable response. The practice of awareness takes us below the reasonableness that we'd

198

|||||||

A
Field
Guide
to
Getting
Lost

like to think we live with and then we start to see something quite fascinating, which is the drama of our inner dialogue, of the stories that go through our minds and the feelings that go through our heart, and we start to see in this territory it isn't so neat and orderly and, dare I say it, safe or reasonable. So in the practice of awareness, which has gone on for centuries after centuries and millennium after millennium, human beings have asked themselves, Hmmmm, how do I engage this process in a way that I don't become too frightened by what it might unfold or too complacent by avoiding it? This is the delicate work of awareness.

"You hear a sound, and you think, that's a big truck going around the corner. It all happens in half a second. We see someone and make up a story about who they are, and sometimes we get ourselves into a lot of trouble with the stories we make up as we weave our world. And the practice of awareness doesn't say don't weave your world. That's what we're hardwired to do, it's not a volitional thing to think 'truck' after hearing that sound. The practice of awareness says don't grasp it too tightly, don't be too convinced. And in that simpler way of being, it's okay to become like the Turtle Man, it's okay to sometimes experience not knowing what to do next, to run into a barrier. It's okay to realize that life has a mysterious quality to it, it has an element of uncertainty, it's okay to realize that we do need help, that calling out for help is a very generous act because it allows others to help us and it allows us to be helped. Sometimes we're calling out for help. Sometimes we're offering help, and then this hostile world becomes a very different place. It is a world where there is help being received and help being given, and in such a world this compelling determined world according to me loses some of its urgency and desperation. It's not so necessary in a generous world, in a world where help is available, to be so adamant about the world according to me."

Several months later, I was camping on the eastern side of the Sierra, in a forest of Jeffrey pines that stood far apart on that pale sand, speaking of vast root systems tapping out what moisture there was in that dry place. The pinecones fell in perfect circles under the trees, and the place seemed almost geometrically pure: the flat plain of volcanic sand, the tall straight trees, the dark circles of cones. In the warmth of day, the bark of these trees gives off a fragrance like vanilla and butterscotch, a sweetness that added to the tranquility of the place that seemed when we were in it as though it was all there was in the world, as though the trees went on forever, as though time, history, obligation were no longer on the map. We slept in our cars on a night so cold that the water in our dishpan was frozen solid by morning. We'd camped there the year before, and that time I'd gotten my car stuck in the sand, several miles from the paved road. It had been a lovely moment to realize that I could count on my traveling companions, and they had gotten me out with good cheer and little fuss. This freezing night I dreamed I'd driven into the backyard of that childhood home and gotten the car

stuck again, but the yard and house belonged to someone else, a middle-aged Asian woman who had added
a second story to it. It was her house now. I wasn't going in, and friends were coming to dislodge the car.

And then as I was preparing to write this chapter, I
dreamed of the place again, from the outside again. We
were burying my father's and grandmother's hearts by
rocky graves like ornamental excrescences around the
edges of the swimming pool. This time the pool had dark
dirt on its bottom, and its sides were no longer straight
but wavering, encrusted with big stones. It was becoming a pond. The dark hearts had been in my refrigerator,
in a Ziploc bag, like butcher's meat. A dream doesn't
have to explain how long they'd been there. Which one
was bigger, my dreaming self wondered, and did the size
indicate generosity, body size, or unhealthy enlargement? Both died of heart trouble. And through a knothole in the tall back fence—and there was a real knothole
I had forgotten, which in real life did look out onto the
hilly pasture of a little quarter horse ranch—I saw horse-
drawn carriages speeding by, then horses galloping faster
and glossier than ever, exuberant with power, with life.

A few months later, I went to spend a few weeks
writing in the county I grew up in, not the suburban corridor whose northernmost edge that house sat upon, but
its wild west, mostly parkland and dairy farms. Geese
were flying south, apples were ripe on the trees, and one
day a naturalist named Rich took me around to look at
birds. While we were watching a pair of white-tailed
kites in the tree they roost in, he mentioned that they had

been thought to be extinct, and they were now doing so well that they were expanding their ecological niche and range. Almost everywhere but the black bands on their wings, the birds were as dazzlingly white as doves, though their contours were the condensed ferocity of hawks. Some people call them angel hawks. We went calling on dozens of shorebirds and waterbirds, a kingfisher, green herons half-hidden in the reeds, one gulping a blue dragonfly still whirring as it went down that long narrow throat, songbirds, and then a turtle peering above the still water of an old millpond. Reflection turned its tilted head in profile into a notched oddity with two yellow-gold eyes looking back at us. We traveled to several places not far from the road, and through this guide's eyes and tales I saw a completely different place than this the one I had been coming back to almost all my life. My place had been made out of plants and landforms and light and some human histories. His was crowded with creatures going about their lives, each living according to a pattern, the patterns interwoven into a tapestry of formidable complexity.

Some ideas are new, but most are only recognition of what has been there all along, the mystery in the middle of the room, the secret in the mirror. Sometimes one unexpected thought becomes the bridge that lets you traverse the country of the familiar in an unprecedented way. You know the the usual story about the world, the one about ongoing encroachment that continues to escalate and thereby continues to wipe out species. Rich told a different story about how here for a hundred years or so after the gold rush the newcomers blasted away at everything that moved, an era that let up half a century ago. And so, he said, in North America at least, a lot of species have come back. In this county with so many miles of open space, he told me, even coyotes became locally extinct. I realized that the hills I roamed as a child were empty and silent compared to what they are now. It was odd to think of what had been my paradise and refuge as an impoverished landscape, though I had long known its very grass wasn't native.

Across the continent many of the common animals are coming back, the deer, moose, bears, coyotes, and cougars, a story that hasn't been made much of. Many of the birds endangered by DDT four or five decades ago have likewise returned, peregrines, eagles, osprey, and more. But in this county, more happened. In the third quarter of the nineteenth century, tule elk were hunted into extinction altogether on this coast, and throughout their California habitat only a few survived. These survivors were discovered in 1874 in a tule marsh in the San Joaquin, the valley the Death Valley Forty-Niners had pronounced as Sand Walking. Their discoverers were in the process of draining the marsh for agriculture. A serious endeavor to save the species began in the twentieth century, and ten animals were reintroduced to this coast the year I left home and the county. Since then they had multiplied into the hundreds, and they are, in the present order of things, safe as a species.

I knew about the elk, but as Rich talked I began to see a picture I had not before, of all the animals who had hovered in the doorway of disappearance and then returned to this place. Elephant seals had vanished for a hundred and fifty years from this stretch of coast and by 1890 vanished from all their breeding grounds but one place in Baja, their numbers dwindled down to about a thousand. Four years after the elk returned, the first breeding pair was sighted here. Now, twenty years later, a couple thousand of them heave themselves up onto this county's remotest beach in winter to quarrel and bask and give birth, and there are altogether about a hundred and fifty thousand of them in the world. Brown pelicans and crested egrets had come back from the brink, as had other waterbirds, and almost half the birds of North America are in this place at least some of the time, up to two hundred species at a time. The place also has a number of unique subspecies, evolved in isolation over tens of thousands of years, and more than a score of endangered and threatened species altogether, including coho salmon spawning in its streams. I had seen them too, golden female and ruby male thrashing their way up shallow water in the early dusk of drizzly midwinter.

After that day, I found a book at the house I was staying at, about how the land on which these creatures flourished was protected from development, and found my father's name in the index. We moved back to California when he was hired to write the master plan for the county, and he spent the next five years working on a document that protects from development most of its western portion that wasn't already under state, federal, or land-trust protection. The drive for protection came

||||||

A
Field
Guide
to
Getting
Lost

from citizens first, and it was their support that made it possible for the professionals to push their plan through, but it was the planners who wrote the rules of this protection and took much of the heat. The book spoke of "a revolutionary Marin Countywide Plan, which used 'designing with nature' as its method for preserving Marin's extraordinary landscapes and preventing its cities from sprawling together." I own a copy of the environmental plan whose title was drawn from a poem by Lew Welch quoted on the flyleaf, "This is the last place. / There is no where else to go," and so it was called *Can the Last Place Last?* So far it has, though Welch didn't. He walked into the Sierra Nevada wilds in 1971, and no trace of him was ever found.

The plan "went through fifty-seven public hearings and was adopted in 1973. . . . The plan was the inspiration of talented county planners Paul Zucker and Al Solnit. Zucker later lost his job after he lost a supervisorial race, and Solnit was the victim of vicious attacks by developers and hostile editorials. But the Plan was embraced by the public and has prevailed through minor revisions for over twenty-five years." One summer evening when I was about nine, my father came home late and found a forgotten glass of chocolate milk gone sour on the kitchen counter. Waste enraged him, and since I was the principal drinker of chocolate milk, he rushed into my room, flicked the light on, and dashed it in my face as I slept, so that I woke up dripping with a giant roaring over me. (That the milk was a brother's is only a detail; it was a very random universe in there.)

Reading that account, I realized that what he had come home from was one of those rancorous meetings at which the fate of this place was being decided.

The house was a small place inside a larger one, or a small story inside a larger one; picture the stories nesting like Russian dolls, so that terrible things were happening in that house, but they were tied to the redemption happening on the larger scale of the county, which was in part reaction to the violent erasures going on across the country and the world. I had left the house for good a quarter of a century before and just gotten out of it in my dreams over the past year, but the county was something I chose to return to again and again, and on this return I'd seen the nesting of those stories, as well as some of the animals that had come back. I revisited the elk a few days before the day of the angel hawks. Most of them live out on the remotest peninsula of this remote place, a spit of land like a north-pointing finger, segregated from the rest of the world by a ten-foot-tall ring of cyclone fencing across its knuckle, a peninsula at whose tip I had realized that the end of the world could be a place as well as a time. They'd been lounging among the grasses and the domelike lupine shrubs, herds of cow elk with a few bulls among them and herds of young bulls who scrambled to their feet at the sound of my approach so that their antlers looked like a forest rising up. The end of the world was wind-scoured but peaceful, black cormorants and red starfish on wavewashed dark rocks below a sandy bluff, and beyond them all the sea spreading far and then farther.

Fuck yeah

Sources

Open Door

Poe: in his "The Daguerreotype," 1840, reprinted in Jane M. Rabb, *Literature and Photography: Interactions 1840–1990* (Albuquerque: University of New Mexico Press, 1995), 5.

Benjamin: in his "A Berlin Chronicle," in Walter Benjamin, *Reflections: Essays, Aphorisms, Autobiographical Writings,* translated by Edmund Jephcott, edited by Peter Demetz (New York: Schocken, 1986).

Boone: is quoted in many places, with many versions of this statement he is said to have made to Chester Harding, who had come to paint the eighty-five-year-old man.

Dorothy Lee: in her 1959 book *Freedom and Culture*.

Native California language preservation and revival: "A Faith in Words," a September 2004 article by Kerry Tremain, in the University of California, Berkeley, alumni magazine, *California Monthly*.

Jaime de Angulo: in the introduction by Bob Callahan to the anthology he edited, *A Jaime de Angulo Reader* (Berkeley: Turtle Island Press, 1979).

The Blue of Distance

Robert Hass: in his poem "Meditations at Lagunitas," in his Ecco Press book *Praise* (1990).

Simone Weil: in the book *Gravity and Grace,* quoted in Francine du Plessix Gray's 2001 Penguin Lives biography of her.

Most of the blue-of-distance paintings described here are in the Louvre, but Da Vinci's portrait is in the National Gallery in Washington, D.C.

Henry Bosse's album: was republished by Twin Palms Press in 2002.

Gary Paul Nabhan: in a 1994 book coauthored by Stephen Trimble, *The Geography of Childhood*.

Daisy Chains

Emptiness is the track: in Stephen Batchelor's 1997 *Buddhism without Beliefs.*

The Blue of Distance

Cabeza de Vaca: from the version translated and edited by Cyclone Covey and published by the University of New Mexico Press (1983).

Eunice Williams: all quotes from John Demos's *The Unredeemed Captive* (1994).

Mary Jemison: in Frances Roe Kestler's 1990 compilation *The Indian Captivity Narrative: A Woman's View.*

Cynthia Ann Parker: from Margaret Schmidt Hacker's 1990 *Cynthia Ann Parker, the Life and the Legend.*

Thomas Jefferson Mayfield: in his account published by Heyday Books and the California Historical Society as *Indian Summer: Traditional Life among the Choinumne Indians of California's San Joaquin Valley,* introduced by Malcolm Margolin.

Pat Barker: in her 1992 novel *Regeneration.*

Abandon

David Wojnarowicz: in his *Close to the Knives: A Memoir of Disintegration* (1991).

The Clash: in their song "London Calling."

The Blue of Distance

"Would You Lay with Me (in a Field of Stone)," written by David Allen Coe.

"Walking After Midnight," written by Don Hecht and Alan Block.

"Long Black Veil," written by Danny Dill and Marijohn Wilkins.

"No Man's Land," written by Bob Dylan.

Isak Dinesen: in "The Young Man with the Carnation" in her *Winter's Tales.*

ııııııı

Two Arrowheads

Vertigo: Madeleine's passage is quoted in Jeff Craft and Aaron Leventhal's *Footsteps in the Fog: Alfred Hitchcock's San Francisco* (2002).

The Blue of Distance

Yves Klein sources include: the 1982 catalogue from the Institute for the Arts at Rice University, *Yves Klein, 1928–1962: A Retrospective,* which includes Thomas McEvilley's spectacular essay; Nicholas Charlet's 2000 book, *Yves Klein,* with a preface by Klein's friend Pierre Restany; and Sidra Stich's 1994 *Yves Klein* volume.

Sources for the map histories include: Peter Whitfield, *New Found Lands:*

Maps in the History of Exploration; R. A. Skleton's 1958 *Explorer's Maps;* Lloyd Arnold Brown's 1949 *The Story of Maps;* John Leighly's 1972 *California as an Island: An Illustrated Essay;* Glen McLaughlin with Nancy H. Ma, *The Mapping of California as an Island,* 1995; and Peter Turchi's 2004 book, *Maps of the Imagination: The Writer as Cartographer,* where I found Jean Baptiste Bourguignon d'Anville quoted.

Slavoj Zizek's response to Donald Rumsfeld: in "On Abu Ghraib," *London Review of Books,* June 3, 2004.

209

One-Story House

Carobeth Laird: in her 1993 memoir *Encounters with an Angry God: Recollections of My Life with John Peabody Harrington* and her *The Chemehuevis* (1976).

William Manly: in his 1977 memoir *Death Valley in '49.*

The talk at San Francisco Zen Center was given by Abbot Paul Haller.

The book that mentioned my father was L. Martin Griffin's 1998 *Saving the Marin-Sonoma Coast.*

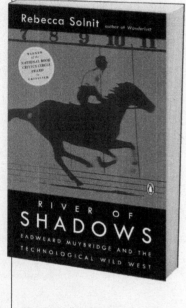

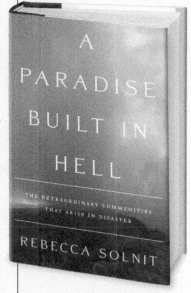